M000309224

the Blonde Vegetarian

EASY COOKING FOR GOOD HEALTH, WEIGHT MANAGEMENT, AND GREAT TASTE

Rebecca Woodland

MEGA
PRODUCTIONS
MADDEN ENTERTAINMENT GROUP ARTISTS

Published and distributed by

94-411 KŌʻAKI STREET, WAIPAHU, HAWAIʻI 96797-2806
ORDERS: (800) 468-2800
INFORMATION: (808) 564-8800
FAX: (808) 564-8877
islandheritage.com

ISBN# : 1-59700-808-7
First Edition, First Printing - 2010

Photography by Roméo Collado
Food styled by Iwa Bush

Copyright ©2010 Island Heritage Publishing

All rights reserved. Printed in Hong Kong. No part of this book may be reproduced, stored in a retrieval system, or transmitted in any form or by any means — electronic, mechanical, photocopy, recording, or any other — except for brief quotations printed in reviews, without prior express permission of the author. Making copies of any part of this book for any purpose other than your own personal use is a violation of United States copyright laws.

For additional information or to order, contact:
Rebecca Woodland
P.O. Box 235457
Honolulu, Hawaii 96823
(808) 282-9866
www.theblondevegetarian.com

DEDICATION

To the survivors,

living proof that this way of eating can
transform and save your life.

And to all of you who have supported me on this journey ~

you know who you are.

❦ ACKNOWLEDGEMENTS ❦

To Clarisse Mau, whose friendship and generosity made this book possible.
Thank you for letting us invade and occupy your beautiful, well-equipped kitchen
(and home) to create and photograph the foods in this book.

To Yolanda Kerr, for reading my writings and insisting they be shared with others.
Thank you for taking the initiative when I wouldn't.

To John Knorek, who forwarded my writing to Dale Madden.
Thank you for making our Island Heritage connection possible.

To the entire staff and creative team of Island Heritage Publishing,
whose innovation and imagination breathed life into the pages of this book.

And to those who believed in me most when it meant the most.

I am forever grateful to all of you.

The Blonde Vegetarian is a practical, easy, comprehensive cookbook designed for everyday use. The recipes are simple and delicious, with thorough, user-friendly explanations. Born from my own cancer ordeal and a family member's battle with heart disease, my commitment to delicious, low-fat vegetarian cooking was a matter of necessity. Our survival depended on it.

When I first started cooking low-fat vegan foods, I had to unlearn and relearn almost everything I knew (or thought I knew) about cooking. I was determined to learn how to create delicious, health-promoting, cancer-fighting meals—no matter what the obstacles. For several months after my cancer surgery, my physical condition made it difficult to chop vegetables or even stir soup, so this determination had to be strong. I was not willing to sacrifice flavor; the food had to taste great or we would not have the incentive to continue eating this way for the rest of our lives.

> **"...I had to unlearn and relearn almost everything I knew (or thought I knew) about cooking."**

I bought dozens of cookbooks and collected countless recipes. As I tried to follow these recipes, I became more and more confused. They assumed I already knew what the ingredients were, where to buy them, and how to prepare them. For example, some recipes called for tofu. They didn't specify what kind (silken? firm? soft?), or tell me what to do with it before I put it in the dish I was preparing. The results were frustrating, expensive, and wasteful. If the recipe told me to press the tofu, it didn't say how. Worse yet, some recipes had instructions that didn't make sense to me. Vegetarian cooking was truly a mystery. How was I ever going to be able to eat this way for the rest of my life if I couldn't even figure out the recipes?

Shopping for ingredients was a bizarre experience. I had no idea what the items looked like or where to find them. I nearly passed out the first time I bought flaxseed oil. Why was it refrigerated, and why did it cost ten times as much as other oils? I thought it must be a mistake. Bulk items in bins totally baffled me. I never knew there were so many varieties of brown rice, and how can you tell the difference between quinoa and millet? Everything looked beige. Different types of flour really confused me, and what was this nutritional yeast stuff? (No, it is not the same as brewer's

yeast.) Where in the store could I find miso? What do you mean, what kind of miso? I didn't realize the variety of foods available.

That was only the beginning of The Great Grocery Shopping Challenge. Reading and understanding nutrition labels required more time and concentration than I ever imagined. I was trying to avoid sugar and hydrogenated oils, but nearly everything contained sugar in some form — or many forms — and hydrogenated/partially hydrogenated oils were in almost all snack foods, including those found in health food stores. I finally gave up and decided not to buy packaged foods.

Once I mastered the art of grocery shopping, I was faced with the formidable challenge of deciphering recipes. Unclear, complicated instructions, vocabulary I didn't understand, techniques I had never heard of — this wasn't working for me. I decided to create my own recipes and write them in such a way that I could understand and follow them. (If I can understand and follow a recipe, anyone can.) I conceived the idea for this cookbook and decided to name it after me, The Blonde Vegetarian.

I hope this book will inspire you to adopt a healthy, lowfat, vegetarian lifestyle and make it easier for you to cook and eat vegetarian foods for the rest of your life.

It is never too late—in fiction or in life—to revise.

—Nancy Thayer

Table of Contents

A WORD FROM THE AUTHOR:

The Blonde Vegetarian is a practical guide for the would-be vegetarian who doesn't quite know where to start. These easy-to-follow recipes and cooking tips show how to make a painless transition to a delicious, healthful, low-fat, plant-based diet without feeling starved or deprived. All recipes have been tested and approved by non-vegetarians and folks who claim they "can't cook"—but they successfully prepared (and thoroughly enjoyed) these recipes.

During my recovery from cancer, I knew I had to take charge of my health and stop taking my body for granted. Following the recommendations of my naturopathic physician, I deleted processed, refined "foods" from my diet. (This included most packaged and canned foods, as well as fast foods.) I also eliminated dairy, eggs, meat, poultry, caffeine, sugar, artificial sweeteners, and hydrogenated oils (trans-fats). They were replaced by a huge variety of whole grains, nuts, legumes, fresh fruits and vegetables, and occasional soy products. A new culinary world opened up to me, and with it a whole new life!

The results were dramatic and almost immediate. While my original intention was to get well and prevent the cancer from recurring, the other benefits were impossible to ignore. Respiration normalized, sinuses cleared, chronic headaches and stomachaches disappeared, energy increased, sleep improved, complexion cleared, and I even lost weight— even though I was eating constantly! I am living proof that a radical change in diet can dramatically improve your health, appearance, and every aspect of your life.

Since then, I have personally witnessed phenomenal improvements in countless people who have followed the recipes and recommendations set forth in this book: heart patients whose condition actually reversed without medication or surgery, diabetics who reduced or eliminated their dependence on insulin injections, asthmatics who no longer required inhalers, people with hypertension whose blood pressure normalized without medication, and so on. While I make no medical claims or guarantees, I am certain this book will help you find your own path toward optimal health.

Every person is faced with different health challenges. I believe each of us has different dietary requirements and limitations, which vary throughout our lives. No single "diet" is perfect for everyone. I am convinced that everyone will benefit from a plant-based, whole foods diet, rich in variety and natural flavor.

As you and your family embark on a more healthful, delicious way of cooking and eating, you will be amazed at the vast array of culinary possibilities. Your taste buds will awaken. Best of all, your health will improve. May this cookbook make your journey toward good health a little easier and a lot more delicious! Bon appétit!

FYI:

Certain terms and ingredients in this book may be unfamiliar; others may require clarification or even substitutions. Please refer to the glossaries at the end of the book for more information about ingredients, utensils, cooking techniques, and terminology.

> *"A new culinary world opened up to me, and with it a whole new life!"*

SALT: means sea salt, Kosher salt, or Hawaiian salt. My favorite is alaea salt, made from coarse Hawaiian salt mixed with red Hawaiian clay. It is a beautiful orange-red color, mineral-rich, and very tasty. I keep it in an airtight ceramic salt grinder, which prevents caking. A few grinds is plenty for most dishes. Avoid table salt (that refined, free-flowing stuff in a box that ends up in most salt shakers). It contains chemical additives and tastes harsh and uninteresting compared with other salts.

PEPPER: means freshly ground black peppercorns. I never use pre-ground pepper in a shaker—it reminds me of stale ashes in an ashtray.

SUCANAT®: a brand name for evaporated cane juice (SUgar CAne NATural), also known as Rapadura. Not quite as sweet as sugar, Sucanat® has a distinctive, mild, pleasantly complex flavor.

BROWN SUGAR: means minimally refined brown cane sugar, not the usual "brown" sugar made by adding the extracted molasses back into refined white sugar. C&H is the only brand I know that still makes the real thing!

TEMPERATURE: means degrees Fahrenheit.

Salads and Dressings

Salads come in every color, size, and shape. The basis of these salads is a variety of vegetables: raw, roasted, or steamed. Partnered with legumes, grains, and/or nuts and dressed or simply drizzled with extra virgin olive oil or a squeeze of fresh lemon or lime, the possibilities are endless—even within severe dietary restrictions. Vary texture by slicing vegetables into matchsticks or cutting them on the diagonal, shredding or dicing them into different sizes, and combining crunchy with creamy or chewy. Adorn with fresh herbs and raw seeds or nuts. Salads may be served as appetizers, side dishes, or even entrées. By combining vegetables with legumes, grains, and/or nuts, a salad becomes a significant source of protein, fiber, vitamins, and minerals. Many of these salads stand on their own as substantial lunches. Try them with different homemade dressings from this book, and you will never again be bored by your salads!

WASHING GREENS AND OTHER VEGETABLES

Scrub vegetables under cool running water to remove excess dirt and pesticides. Fill a large bowl with cool water. Submerge greens in water several times. Remove greens from water with your hands (Do NOT pour the dirty water over the greens!), then dump out the water. Refill bowl with fresh water and repeat procedure until there is no more sand or dirt at the bottom of the bowl. This may require several washings. A set of white plastic nesting bowls is helpful, because the sediment will be more visible and you will have extra bowls to hold the greens while refilling the washing bowl. Make sure you thoroughly wash ALL greens and vegetables, even if they are supposedly pre-washed. Parsley and broccoli are among the most difficult and time-consuming vegetables to get completely sediment-free. Although it may seem inefficient, it is best to wash vegetables just before using. They stay fresher longer when they have not been washed ahead of time.

Raw Garden Salad

Serves 8-10

Preparation time: variable, depending on types of vegetables selected

Bursting with nutrients and flavor, this colorful salad is as varied as your imagination. Use seasonal produce if possible and scrub everything thoroughly even if it "looks" clean. Vary ingredients according to taste preferences and vegetable availability. This recipe makes enough to feed a large family, so be sure to downsize the recipe if preparing it for fewer people. If making more than you can eat at one meal, store the undressed salad in an airtight container and refrigerate. Eat within two days.

Choose smaller zucchini with firm flesh and unblemished skin. Zucchini turns bitter and the seeds toughen as it grows larger.

1	small zucchini (green or yellow), diced		1	c. alfalfa or clover sprouts
1	small beet, peeled and diced		½	c. cucumber, chopped
1	medium carrot, chopped		½	c. daikon radish or turnip, diced (optional)
1	c. broccoli, cut into bite-size pieces		½	c. red cabbage, shredded
1	stalk celery, leaves included, chopped		½	c. avocado, diced
1	c. green cabbage or won bok, shredded		¼	c. watercress or parsley, chopped
1	c. romaine lettuce, torn			pumpkin seeds or sunflower seeds (optional topping)

1. Dice, shred, or chop into bite-size pieces about 10 to 12 c. of vegetables.
2. Toss all vegetables together in large bowl and dress with VERY EASY DRESSING or any other dressing in this book.
3. Top with your choice of raw sunflower seeds or pumpkin seeds.

ABOUT DRESSINGS

Dressing up vegetables is an art. Almost all commercially-prepared dressings contain a huge percentage of sugars (often disguised as corn syrup), vinegars, and low-quality oils. Most have preservatives which can produce nasty side-effects in some people. The recipes in this book use lemon or lime juice (always freshly-squeezed, of course!) and good-quality vinegars, and the oils are all expeller-cold-pressed. Flaxseed oil is an excellent source of Omega-3 fatty acids, essential to everyone's health. Liberal use of aromatic herbs provides flavor and vitamins. You'll never want to revert to using store-bought dressings! NEVER use bottled or reconstituted lemon juice in these recipes! Flavor will be seriously altered and nutritional value will be compromised.

Very Easy Dressing 1

extra virgin olive oil
fresh or dried herbs (oregano,
      thyme, basil, parsley, or dill)

salt and pepper to taste

Drizzle a little olive oil over greens or vegetables or whole grain salads. Add a pinch of fresh or dried herbs and add a sprinkle of salt and coarsely ground pepper.

Very Easy Dressing 2

lemon or lime juice
fresh herbs

salt to taste

Squeeze fresh lemon or lime juice onto greens, vegetables, or whole grains. Add fresh herbs (cilantro or dill go great with lime), a sprinkle of salt, and enjoy a burst of summertime flavor.

Carrot Slaw with Dried Cranberries   Serves 4

Preparation time: 10 minutes or less

This is so easy it hardly deserves to be called a recipe. The secret is to use very fresh, sweet carrots and fresh (not bottled) lemon juice. The cranberries add a festive touch and a hint of sweet-tartness and the mint provides a refreshing contrast. A great source of beta-carotene, vitamin C, and fiber!

3	medium carrots, coarsely grated	Juice of 2-3 lemons (⅓ c.)
⅓	c. dried cranberries	1 Tbsp. mint, chopped, plus mint sprigs for garnish

1. Scrub and peel, carrots before grating. "Fork," see page 14, lemon and squeeze juice onto grated carrots. (This prevents them from turning brown.)
2. Sprinkle in dried cranberries. Add chopped mint. Toss well. Add more lemon juice, if desired.
3. Serve in individual bowls or stemware and garnish with a sprig of fresh mint, if desired.

VARIATION: Use plump raisins instead of dried cranberries.

Cabbage-Carrot-Fennel Slaw

Serves 4

Preparation time: 45 minutes, including "resting" time

With an unusual combination of flavors and textures, this slaw is high in beta-carotene, Vitamin C, and folic acid. The fennel adds a hint of licorice. For a milder flavor and more crunch, or if you can't find fennel, substitute jicama or water chestnuts. Experiment with other salad dressings in this book. Be adventurous!

1	fennel bulb, minced	1	stalk celery, diced
¼	head green cabbage, shredded	2	Tbsp. purple onion, minced
1	large carrot, coarsely grated		
1	c. parsley (½ bunch), chopped	1	Tbsp. scallions or chives, chopped

1. Cut feathery leaves and tough stalks from top of fennel, leaving only the bulb. (Save feathery leaves to add to other salads.) Cut bulb in quarters, remove core, mince finely, and place in medium bowl.
2. Add remaining ingredients to the bowl.
3. Toss with Ginger-Lime-Dill Dressing. Allow to sit at least 20 minutes to meld flavors.

Carrots were first cultivated in the 7th century in Afghanistan. The original carrots were purple. In the 16th century, Dutch horticulturalists developed the orange carrot.

HOW TO FORK A LEMON (OR LIME)

Because fresh lemon and lime juice appear in so many recipes, here is a helpful hint to make things easier. Slice a lemon in half across the "equator." Remove any visible seeds. Stab a fork into cut center and cup the lemon in your other hand. Over the bowl, squeeze the lemon around the fork while twisting the fork inside lemon. Continue until the juice is all squeezed out. Discard rind and remove any stray seeds with the fork. This method is also recommended for squeezing limes.

Ginger-Lime-Dill Dressing

Yield: about 1 cup

Preparation time: less than 10 minutes

This zesty dressing is fabulous with quinoa salad as well as other whole-grain salads. Try it on lightly steamed vegetables or green salads.

⅓	c. fresh lime juice (about 4 limes)		2	tsp. fresh ginger root, peeled and finely minced
¼	c. Barlean's flaxseed oil		2	tsp. dried dill weed or chopped fresh dill
¼	c. extra virgin olive oil			dash Tabasco or chili sauce
½	tsp. salt			

1. In jar or bottle with tight-fitting lid, combine all ingredients. Replace lid tightly and shake well. Shake again just before using. This dressing keeps for up to 1 week in the refrigerator.

VARIATION: For a completely different flavor, use up to 1 tsp. ground cumin instead of ginger.

Quinoa Salad with Ginger-Lime-Dill Dressing

Serves 6-8

Preparation and cooking time: 30 minutes

A surprising combination of flavors, this unusual salad is high in protein, fiber, Omega-3 fatty acids, and calcium. The special dressing makes the salad.

1	c. quinoa		¼	tsp. salt
1½	c. boiling water		¼	c. nuts (slivered almonds walnuts, or pistachios), chopped
¼	c. raisins			
¼	c. dried apricots, chopped		¼	c. bell pepper, diced (red, yellow, orange, green, or combination), chopped

1. Rinse quinoa under cool running water. Rinse again until water runs clear. Do NOT skip this step or quinoa will be disgustingly bitter!!
2. In large pot with lid, bring water to rolling boil. Stir in rinsed quinoa and add salt. Turn heat to simmer and cover pot. Cook quinoa for about 15 to 20 minutes, or until liquid evaporates and little spirals appear on the quinoa. (Quinoa should not be mushy. Each grain should still be separate.) Remove from heat and fluff lightly with fork. Let it cool, uncovered.
3. Meanwhile, combine all remaining ingredients in mixing bowl.
4. Add cooled cooked quinoa to bowl. Drizzle it with Ginger-Lime-Dill Dressing. Toss gently to "fluff." Refrigerate for several hours to allow flavors to mingle. Serve on a bed of romaine.

Basic Green Salad

Serves 6-20 (depending on choice of ingredients)

Preparation time: variable, depending on vegetables

Try any combination of textures and flavors to create your own green salad magic! Here are some suggestions to nudge you out of your green salad doldrums. Iceberg lettuce is not included, as it has minimal flavor and almost no nutritional value. Do not make more than can be eaten at one meal. Freshness is imperative for optimal flavor, nutrition, texture, and appearance.

1. Allowing 1½ c. per person, wash, dry, and tear or cut into bite-size pieces any combination of:

MILD GREENS:	TANGY GREENS:
Bibb lettuce	arugula
romaine	watercress
Boston lettuce	chicory
red-leaf lettuce	escarole
Manoa lettuce	Belgian endive

2. Place in large serving bowl and add any amount or combination of:

SPROUTS:	FRESH HERBS:	ONIONS:
alfalfa clover	basil	chives
mung bean	parsley	scallions
lentil	cilantro	shallots
broccoli	dill	Maui (or sweet)
pea	oregano	purple
soybean	tarragon	

3. Dress with your favorite dressing from this book and add some other goodies such as:

garbanzo beans	walnuts	almonds
pumpkin seeds	sunflower seeds	pecans

4. Toss with dressing to coat evenly, and enjoy immediately!

Creamy Tropical Dressing

Yield: 1 cup

Preparation time: 5 minutes or less

Lightly sweet and creamy, this simple dressing works well with most slaws, green salads, and fruit salads.

¾ c. Vegenaise® or Nayonaise (or other eggless mayonnaise)
2   Tbsp. orange juice (juice from ½ orange)
2   Tbsp. pineapple juice (or liquid from canned pineapple)

In pint jar with tight-fitting lid, combine all ingredients. Shake very well. Add more juice, if desired. Pour over salad and toss gently.

Tropical Coleslaw

Serves 6-8

Preparation time: 15 minutes

Colorful, flavorful, and loaded with vitamin C, this crunchy slaw has a tropical twist and festive flair.

1	red cabbage (about 3 c.), shredded	¼	c. dried papaya or mango, diced
1	green cabbage (about 3 c.), shredded	¾	c. pineapple chunks, canned or fresh
¼	c. dried cranberries (or more for garnish)	¼	c. walnuts, pecans, pistachios, or macadamia nuts

1. Finely shred equal parts green and red cabbage. Pour into large serving bowl.
2. Add dried cranberries (Craisins or Mariani brand recommended), dried papaya or mango, pineapple, and nuts. Toss gently.
3. Pour Creamy Tropical Dressing over slaw and toss well. Garnish with a sprinkle of dried cranberries or nuts.

Tomato Salad

Serves 4-6

Preparation time: 10 minutes

Resting time: 30 minutes

Deceptively simple, this salad sparkles with flavor and color. Any kind of fresh, perfectly ripe tomatoes may be substituted. If available, heirloom tomatoes or yellow tomatoes are good choices. Allow at least thirty minutes resting time for flavors to marry. (Don't skip this step!)

3-4	ripe tomatoes, sliced	1	Tbsp. balsamic vinegar
¼	c. oil-packed sun-dried tomatoes, chopped	1	Tbsp. extra virgin olive oil
zest of 1 lemon		salt	
2	Tbsp. fresh basil, chiffonaded	pepper	

1. Arrange sliced tomatoes artfully on serving platter.
2. Sprinkle sun-dried tomatoes over other tomatoes on platter.
3. Chiffonade fresh basil (stack leaves, roll them tightly, and slice into ribbons). Sprinkle lemon zest and basil on top of tomatoes.
4. Drizzle liberally with balsamic vinegar and extra virgin olive oil. Salt to taste. Add a few grinds of coarsely ground black pepper to finish.
5. Let salad rest for 30 minutes before serving to allow flavors to meld.

Middle Eastern Tabouli

Serves 6-8

Preparation time: 30 minutes

Light and nutty-tasting bulgur (pre-cooked, dried, cracked wheat) is the backbone of classic tabouli. Loaded with flavor, color and texture, this dish works well as a salad, side dish, or entrée. Feel free to increase amounts of herbs or add other vegetables if you wish.

1	c. raw bulgur		1	bunch fresh mint, chopped
1¼	c. water		1	bunch parsley, chopped
2	garlic cloves, minced		10	basil leaves, chiffonaded (optional)
1	cucumber, diced		¾	c. garbanzo beans, drained and rinsed (optional)
¼	c. purple onion, diced		½	tsp. salt
2	tomatoes, diced (Roma preferred)		1	large lemon (at least 3 Tbsp. juice)
1	red or yellow bell pepper, diced		1	Tbsp. extra virgin olive oil (or more, if desired)

1. Bring water to boil. Pour over bulgur. Let sit for 20 minutes or until all water is absorbed.
2. Add all remaining ingredients except olive oil. Drizzle with olive oil immediately before serving. For a more authentic dish, add extra parsley and mint. Adjust seasonings.
3. Toss and serve on a bed of greens, garnished with cherry tomatoes, red bell pepper rings, or purple onion rings.

Sharpen your knives and use the right knife for the job. Buy several good polyethylene cutting boards and flexible cutting mats. To keep a cutting board from slipping while cutting on it, place a piece of sticky mat (often sold in rolls and used for lining shelves) on the counter before putting the cutting board down. This creates a slight "cushion" which helps prevent carpal tunnel pain caused by repetitive chopping on a hard surface. This also keeps knives from dulling too quickly. Remember to wash cutting boards in the dishwasher frequently, as they become a breeding ground for molds and bacteria if not thoroughly cleaned and dried before storing.

Tomato-Corn Salad

Serves 6-8

Preparation time: 10 minutes

This festive, simple salad is delicious with fresh corn, but works well (and is quicker) with canned corn. The sweetness of the corn contrasts dramatically with the tartness of lime and the pungency of cilantro and onion. A feast for the eyes and the palate, this salad is basically Garden Salsa with corn kernels.

3	(11 oz.) cans whole kernel corn, drained	1	bunch cilantro, chopped
⅓	c. purple onion, diced	2-3	Tbsp. lime juice (2 large limes)
1	large ripe tomato (or 3 Roma tomatoes), diced	¼	tsp. salt (optional) cilantro sprigs for garnish

1. Pour corn into glass serving bowl. (This salad looks best in a transparent bowl.)
2. Add onion and tomato. Add chopped cilantro to bowl. (Amount of each ingredient may be adjusted to suit personal tastes.)
3. Squeeze lime juice over everything. Add salt and toss gently. Garnish with cilantro sprigs, if desired.

VARIATION: Add red bell pepper and/or jalapeño pepper (seeded and diced). If corn is in season, use fresh corn instead of canned. If desired, add more fresh lime juice. NEVER use bottled or reconstituted lime juice!

Broccoli-Tomato Salad

Serves 4-6

Preparation and cooking time: 15 minutes

This bright salad bursts with flavor and vitamins! If perfectly ripe tomatoes are not available, don't make this salad.

1	large head broccoli, cut into bite-size pieces	2	Tbsp. extra virgin olive oil
2	ripe tomatoes, diced		salt
1	Tbsp. red wine vinegar or rice vinegar		pepper

1. Bring water to boil in large pot (fill about half-way). Bring water to boil. Add ½ tsp. salt after water begins to boil.
2. Meanwhile, thoroughly wash broccoli. Peel stems. Cut into bit-size pieces.
3. Blanch broccoli in boiling water (about 1 minute). Do NOT overcook!
4. With slotted spoon or strainer, remove blanched broccoli from pot and immerse in bowl of ice water to chill and stop the cooking process. Add more ice, if necessary. When broccoli has cooled, remove from ice water and put in serving bowl.
5. Add tomatoes.
6. Combine vinegar, olive oil, salt, and pepper, mixing well. Pour over vegetables, toss gently, and serve immediately.

Rice Tabouli

Serves 6-8

Preparation time: 20 minutes

A feast for the senses, this hearty, colorful salad is a jazzed up version of classic Middle Eastern tabouli, substituting brown rice for bulgur. A meal in itself, rice tabouli is ideal for potlucks, lunch, or dinner on a hot day. For smaller households, cut the recipe in half so you won't have lots of leftovers. This dish is best served the same day it's made.

1	medium carrot, coarsely grated	1	bunch parsley, chopped
1	red or yellow bell pepper, diced	¾	c. garbanzo beans, drained and rinsed (optional)
1	cucumber, diced	½	tsp. salt
¼	c. purple onion, diced	3	c. cooked brown rice (cook 1¼ c. raw rice in 2 c. water)
2	tomatoes, diced (Roma preferred)		
1-2	Tbsp. extra virgin olive oil	1-2	large lemons (at least ¼ c. juice)
1	bunch fresh mint, chopped		

1. In large serving bowl, combine everything except lemon juice.

2. Just before serving, fork lemon and squeeze over everything. (Do not use bottled or reconstituted lemon juice!) Toss again. Serve at room temperature.

VARIATIONS: Try this with different varieties and combinations of rice (basmati, jasmine, wild rice) but do not use sticky rice or processed rice (e.g. Minute Rice, Uncle Ben's). Lundberg's wild rice blend may be substituted.

Mexican Rice Tabouli

Serves 6-8

Preparation time: 15 minutes

An interesting variation of the previous recipes, this main-dish salad appeals to cilantro lovers. If you can't stand cilantro (most people are passionate about it, one way or the other), omit it. If you enjoy cilantro, add more! Serve with your favorite fresh salsa to kick it up a notch.

3	c. cooked long-grain brown rice	¾	c. black beans, drained and rinsed
1	small zucchini (green or yellow), diced	½	tsp. cumin powder
½	purple onion, chopped	½	tsp. garlic salt
1	cucumber, diced	¼	tsp. crushed dried chile pepper
3	tomatoes (Roma recommended), diced	1	bunch cilantro, chopped
½	c. corn (fresh, canned, or frozen)	1	ripe avocado, diced
1	bell pepper (any color), seeded and diced	¼	c. fresh lime juice (about 3 limes)

1. Combine first 7 ingredients in large bowl. Toss gently.
2. Add black beans, cumin, garlic salt, and chili pepper.
3. Over bowl, fork limes and squeeze juice (about ¼ c. juice) over everything. Toss. Adjust seasoning.
4. Just before serving, add avocado and cilantro and toss again. Serve on a bed of romaine, if desired. Garnish with cilantro, cherry tomato halves, or avocado slices.

VARIATION: For zestier tabouli, add several scoops of Garden Salsa and toss gently.

Chili peppers get the endorphins in your body going, can boost metabolism by 25%, and are loaded with Vitamin C.

Romaine-Watercress Salad with Feta & Walnuts

Serves 4-6

Preparation time: 15 minutes

Watercress adds a spicy punch to this fabulous salad. Walnuts and feta provide protein and texture variations. Feta cheese made with sheep's milk is usually available at Costco. Cheeses made with cow's milk are not recommended for any recipe in this cookbook.

1	head romaine lettuce, torn into bite-size pieces	½	c. feta cheese (made with sheep's milk), crumbled
1	c. watercress, cut into 1-inch pieces	¼	purple onion, sliced (optional)
½	Japanese cucumber, thinly sliced		balsamic vinaigrette or other vinaigrette
½	c. toasted walnut pieces		

1. In large bowl, combine all ingredients except vinaigrette. Toss gently.
2. Dress with balsamic vinaigrette (substitute balsamic vinegar for lemon juice in Basic Easy Vinaigrette) or any dressing in this book. (Optional: Garnish with purple onion rings.)

Basic Easy Vinaigrette

Yield: 1 cup

Preparation time: 5 minutes or less

Versatile and simple to make, this delicious vinaigrette is infinitely adaptable.

⅓	c. extra virgin olive oil	1	tsp. oregano (optional)
⅓	c. Barlean's flaxseed oil	½	tsp. honey or agave nectar (optional)
1	Tbsp. Dijon mustard	¼	tsp. salt (or to taste)
⅓	c. fresh lemon juice or good quality vinegar		

1. Briefly blend all ingredients (in blender or using hand-held immersion blender) for about 3 seconds.
2. Pour over salads or cooked vegetables. Store remainder in tightly-covered bottle in refrigerator.

VARIATIONS: Substitute lime juice for lemon juice. If preferred, substitute extra virgin olive oil for flaxseed oil. Add fresh or dried dill instead of oregano. A handful of chives, fresh parsley, or other leafy herbs may also be substituted. For cilantro-lovers, add a handful of cilantro leaves (to taste). For a creamy dressing with a different taste, add 2 to 3 Tbsp. tahini or well-cooked rice before blending.

HINT: Experiment with various kinds of vinegar for a change. Red wine vinegar, balsamic vinegar, rice wine vinegar, apple cider vinegar, and various herb-flavored vinegars are excellent choices. Avoid eating distilled white vinegar. Save it for cleaning windows and mirrors.

ABOUT FLAXSEED OIL

Flaxseed is high in Omega-3 fatty acid (alpha linolenic acid) and boron. Once the seed coat has been broken it becomes rancid very quickly, so ground flaxseeds and flaxseed oil must be kept in the freezer or refrigerator. Buy a small amount, only what you plan to use within a couple of weeks. I recommend Barlean's flaxseed oil because I believe it tastes much better than any other brand, and is highly nutritious. If this is the first time you are using flaxseed oil, please make every effort to use Barlean's, or you may be turned off flaxseed oil. Look in the refrigerator section and don't be shocked by the price. It's worth it! Flaxseed oil is considered a supplement. Flaxseed oil must NEVER be used for frying. Use only as a dressing.

Creamy Vinaigrette

To Basic Easy Vinaigrette add up to ¼ c. nonfat plain yogurt or goat cheese or sheep's milk feta or tofu. Blend until very creamy. For added color and flavor, add 1 Tbsp. sun-dried tomatoes (oil-packed) or 1 small chipotle chili (a type of smoked hot chili pepper) before blending.

Creamy Chèvre Herb Dressing   Yield: about 1 cup

Preparation time: 5 minutes

Fresh goat cheese gives this easy dressing its creamy texture and complex flavor. Try using different fresh herbs to suit your taste. Terrific on salads, steamed vegetables, cooked grains, or as a dip for crudités, this dressing is high in magnesium and calcium.

½	c. extra virgin olive oil	½	c. fresh herbs (tarragon, thyme, dill, parsley,
¼	c. fresh lemon juice		cilantro or chives), chopped
2-3	Tbsp. plain fresh goat cheese (chèvre)		

Combine all ingredients in blender. Blend about 15 seconds, until creamy.

VARIATION: Experiment with different fresh herbs, using whatever amounts you choose.

(Note: Do not use flavored goat cheese because this contains additives such as corn syrup solids, a form of sugar. Costco sells delicious plain goat cheese.)

Spinach Salad with Pears, Feta, & Toasted Pecans

Serves 4-6

Preparation time: 15 minutes

Flavorful and appealing, this quick, simple salad uses pre-washed baby spinach and canned pears. Toast pecans in the oven ahead of time and keep them on hand for future recipes.

8	c. baby spinach, pre-washed	½	c. toasted pecans
1	(15 oz.) can sliced pears, drained	1-2	Tbsp. extra virgin olive oil
¾	c. feta cheese (sheep's milk preferred)	2	tsp. balsamic vinegar

1. Pour baby spinach leaves into large bowl. Add pear slices to bowl, reserving 6 slices for garnish.
2. Crumble feta cheese over everything. Add toasted pecans. Toss gently.
3. Drizzle lightly with extra virgin olive oil. Add a splash of balsamic vinegar. Toss again.
4. Arrange reserved pear slices on top.

VARIATION: Goat cheese (chèvre) may be substituted for feta. Raspberry vinaigrette may be substituted for olive oil and balsamic vinegar.

Mixed Greens with Strawberries, Feta, & Almonds

Serves 6

Preparation time: 15 minutes

Vibrant colors, varied textures, and vivid flavors make this salad a favorite during strawberry season. To save time, use pre-washed packaged baby greens (sometimes called spring mix or mesclun). Use only the best quality extra virgin olive oil to dress this simple salad. Do not wash berries until just before using, as they deteriorate very rapidly when exposed to water.

8	c. baby greens (spring mix)	½	c. feta cheese (preferably made with sheep's milk)
1	c. (or less) fresh strawberries, sliced	2-3	Tbsp. slivered almonds
1	bunch fresh mint (about ¼ c.), torn	1-2	Tbsp. extra virgin olive oil

1. Thoroughly wash fresh strawberries. Remove green tops and core. Slice lengthwise into "hearts."
2. Pour pre-washed baby greens into large transparent bowl. Add slivered almonds and fresh mint.
3. Crumble feta cheese over everything.
4. Drizzle lightly with extra virgin olive oil. Toss gently and enjoy immediately!

VARIATIONS: If strawberries are not in season, substitute a can of mandarin orange segments (drained). Toasted pecans or walnut pieces may be substituted for almonds. Baby spinach may be substituted for other greens.

Cilantro-Sesame Pesto Dressing

Yield: ¾ cup

Preparation time: 5 minutes

Perfect for pasta, bean thread noodles, grains and salads, this unusual dressing is a surprise for the taste buds!

1-2	Tbsp. ginger root, peeled and chopped	1	garlic clove, peeled and mashed
½	c. cilantro, coarsely chopped	2	tsp. dark sesame oil
½	c. green onion or chives, coarsely chopped	¼-½	tsp. salt (to taste)
¼	c. olive oil or expeller-pressed canola oil	¼	tsp. pepper

Put all ingredients in blender. Blend about 20 seconds or until herbs are pulverized to your satisfaction.

VARIATION: Add handful of walnuts or pine nuts to blender and blend until nuts are ground up sufficiently. For use in Asian dishes, substitute sesame oil for all or part of the olive oil.

Greek Country Salad (Horiatiki)

Serves 4

Preparation time: 5 minutes per serving

Simple, intense, and authentic, this beautiful salad should only be made with the ripest, freshest tomatoes and the best-quality extra virgin olive oil (dark greenish is best). Do yourself a favor and use good sheep's-milk feta cheese (not the pre-crumbled stuff).

2-3	tomatoes (ripe and firm), cut into wedges	4	oz. feta cheese, cubed
1	cucumber, thickly sliced or cut into chunks	12-20	Kalamata olives, pitted
1	green or red bell pepper, cut into strips or rings	1	tsp. dried oregano
1	small purple onion, cut into rings	2	Tbsp. extra virgin olive oil

1. Arrange everything except oregano and olive oil on serving plate or combine in large bowl.
2. Sprinkle with oregano. Garnish with more purple onion rings, if desired.
3. Drizzle extra virgin olive oil over everything. Enjoy!

VARIATION: If you want to "stretch" this salad, add romaine to the mix and toss gently. A squeeze of fresh lemon or a splash of balsamic vinegar or red wine vinegar may be added to this version.

> Olives have been cultivated for over 6,000 years. Olive trees can live over 2,000 years. 90% of all olives are used to make olive oil.

Stuffed Avocado Unlimited

1 avocado serves 2 people

Preparation time: varies, depends on type of filling

Fabulous, fancy, and easy, this is an excellent way to serve any salad from this book.

Select 1 perfectly ripe avocado. Remove pit. Stuff avocado with any salad in this book. Serve on a bed of romaine or baby greens. Especially good filled with slaws, whole grains, and bean-based salads.

Multi-Grain Zucchini Salad

Serves 4

Preparation and cooking time: 50 minutes

Chill time: at least 1 hour

This easy main-course salad should be made a few hours ahead. Perfect for potluck, this unusual combination of earthy textures and bright flavors can be served plain or with any dressing from this book. For a shortcut, cook Lundberg's wild rice blend (1 cup uncooked) instead of the mixed grains.

½	c. brown rice	½	c. nuts, chopped (walnuts, pecans, or hazelnuts)
¼	c. pearl barley OR spelt kernels		
2	Tbsp. wild rice or black rice	1	tsp. dill weed (fresh or dried)
1¼	c. water	¼	c. fresh parsley, chopped
1	medium cucumber, peeled and diced	2	Tbsp. extra virgin olive oil
2	small zucchini, diced		salt and pepper
3	Tbsp. lemon juice (1 lemon)		

1. Place grains in 2-quart pot or automatic rice cooker and rinse thoroughly under cool running water until water in pot is clear.
2. Drain, cover with 1¼ c. water. Add ½ tsp. salt. Bring to boil, cover, and reduce heat to simmer. Cook until all liquid is absorbed (about 35 minutes, but do not allow to get mushy). Remove from heat, fluff with fork, and let cool to room temperature.
3. Add cucumber and zucchini to cooked chilled grains. Toss gently.
4. Add dill, parsley, lemon juice, olive oil, and nuts. Toss again. Sprinkle a little salt and pepper to taste.
5. Serve plain or on a bed of leafy greens.
6. Immediately before serving, drizzle a few drops of extra virgin olive oil on top. For a completely different flavor and texture, toss with Tzatziki or Tahini-Dill Dressing instead.

Tahini-Dill Dressing

Yield: almost 1½ cups

Preparation time: 5 minutes

Delicious on plain cooked whole grains, vegetables, and grain-based salads, this dressing provides protein and calcium as well as flavor.

⅓	c. tahini (sesame paste)	½-1	tsp. dark sesame oil
¾	c. water	2	Tbsp. fresh dill (or 2 tsp. dried)
¼-½	tsp. salt		

1. Put all ingredients in blender. Blend until creamy smooth.
2. Serve over whole grains, steamed veggies, salads, etc. Store remainder in tightly sealed bottle in refrigerator and use within several days.

VARIATION: Substitute parsley or cilantro for dill. Use dash of Bragg Liquid Aminos instead of salt. To increase nutritional value, add 2 Tbsp. Barlean's flaxseed oil. Experiment!

Warm Potato-Green Bean Salad

Serves 4-6

Preparation and cooking time: 30 minutes

A mayonnaise-free potato salad enhanced with garlic, this salad is best served warm or at room temperature. For best results, use new potatoes and fresh green beans. It also makes a great side dish, and it tastes even better the next day.

½	lb. new red or Yukon Gold potatoes, cubed	10	garlic cloves, smashed
½	lb. green beans (about 2 c.), cut into 1-inch pieces	2	tsp. Bragg Liquid Aminos
		1	c. water

1. Scrub potatoes. Do not peel. Cut into ¾-inch cubes.
2. Wash and trim green beans before cutting.
3. Smash garlic cloves with the flat surface of knife blade. Remove papery outer covering.
4. In pressure cooker or large nonstick pot with tight-fitting lid, layer potatoes, beans, and garlic. Squirt Bragg Liquid Aminos into water and pour over everything. Cover and cook until potatoes are tender but not mushy (time varies, depending on type of potato and cookware). If using pressure cooker, follow directions for pressure cooking. Lower the heat immediately when pressure builds up and pot starts "whistling" loudly.
5. When potatoes are tender, scoop out potatoes and green beans with slotted spoon and place in serving bowl. Scrape the broth and cooked garlic into blender.

Dressing for this salad:

2	Tbsp. extra virgin olive oil	2	Tbsp. water
1	Tbsp. rice vinegar		pepper (a few grinds)
1	Tbsp. Dijon mustard	¼	tsp. salt

broth and garlic from cooked potato mixture

Blend until creamy. Pour over warm potatoes and beans. Top with freshly-ground pepper.

Mock Egg Salad

Serves 4

Preparation time: 20 minutes, or 5 minutes if tofu has been drained

Easy and versatile, this high-protein "egg" salad can be used to stuff pita bread or as a sandwich filling, or spread on crackers or bagels. Or serve on a bed of greens and garnish with cherry tomato halves and a sprig of parsley.

1	box firm or extra-firm tofu	⅛	tsp. turmeric
2	Tbsp. nutritional yeast flakes	1	Tbsp. red bell pepper, diced or minced
2	tsp. Dijon mustard		pepper (a few grinds)
¼	tsp. salt	1	Tbsp. fresh herbs (chives, dill, or basil), chopped

1. Drain tofu in cotton tea-towel. Let sit for 10 to 15 minutes until towel is completely saturated. Unwrap.
2. Mash tofu with fork. Add nutritional yeast flakes, Dijon mustard, salt, turmeric, and a few grinds of pepper. Mix thoroughly. Add more nutritional yeast if mixture seems too mushy.
3. Add red bell pepper, chives, fresh dill or basil, according to taste. Adjust seasoning.

31

Couscous with Artichoke Hearts

Serves 4-6

Preparation time: 15 minutes

Quick and easy, this can be served as a salad, side dish, or entrée for a light lunch. High in fiber and Omega-3 fatty acids, it is full of surprises in flavor and texture.

1	(14 oz.) can quartered artichoke hearts
1½	c. dry couscous
½	tsp. salt
1	garlic clove, minced
1	Tbsp. fresh dill, chopped (or 1 tsp. dried)
½	c. parsley, chopped
¼	c. scallions or chives, chopped (optional)

⅓	c. lemon juice
⅓	c. walnut pieces
1	Tbsp. Barlean's flaxseed oil
1	Tbsp. extra virgin olive oil

salt and pepper

greens (leaf lettuce, spinach, romaine, or baby greens)

parsley for garnish (optional)

1. Drain artichokes. Reserve liquid and add enough water to liquid to make 1 c. Bring liquid to boil.
2. In heat-proof bowl, place couscous and salt. Pour boiled liquid over couscous, cover and set aside for 5 minutes.
3. Stir garlic, dill, parsley, and scallions into prepared couscous. Add lemon juice, artichoke hearts, walnut pieces, salt and pepper.
4. Just before serving, stir in flaxseed oil and olive oil. Adjust seasoning and add more lemon juice, if desired. Toss lightly. Serve at room temperature on a bed of greens. Garnish with parsley or Gremolata, if desired.

Couscous is a form of pasta made by steaming and then drying cracked durum wheat.

Cranberry Sauce Salad with Celery, Apple, & Walnuts

Serves 12

Preparation time: 10 minutes

A sparkling accompaniment to any holiday feast, this festive salad replaces the familiar cranberry sauce condiment on your holiday table.

1	can whole-berry cranberry sauce
1	apple—Fuji, Granny Smith, or Braeburn (Delicious variety will not work), cored and diced
2	celery stalks, with leaves, diced
½	c. walnuts or pecans, coarsely chopped

Combine all ingredients in medium bowl. Mix everything together with fork. Chill and serve.

Warm Bean Salad with Basil & Goat Cheese

Serves 4-6

Preparation time: 10 minutes

Simple and satisfying, this unusual salad may be made with any kind of large white or pale green bean. Lima, fava, Great Northern, or butter beans may be used. Navy beans or black-eyed peas are another option. Do not use kidney beans or black beans!

1 (15 oz.) can lima or Great Northern beans	10-15 fresh basil leaves, chiffonaded
2 Tbsp. extra virgin olive oil	¼ c. lemon juice (about 1 lemon)
1 garlic clove, minced	salt and pepper
½ c. fresh goat cheese (chèvre) or sheep's milk feta	

1. Pour entire can of beans (including liquid) into saucepan and warm over medium heat (2 to 3 minutes). If you prefer, use 2 c. cooked white beans instead of canned beans. Remove from heat when warm.
2. Using slotted spoon, remove warmed beans from pot (discard liquid). Place in serving bowl. Add garlic. Drizzle with olive oil and fresh lemon juice.
3. Crumble goat cheese (or feta) over everything. Stack basil leaves, roll tightly, and slice into thin ribbons across center vein with a very sharp knife. (This is called "chiffonade.")
4. Just before serving, add basil and stir gently to combine. Add freshly ground pepper and salt if you wish. Serve warm or at room temperature.

There are over one thousand different types of legumes worldwide. Legumes provide an economical source of protein, fiber, folate, and minerals. Garbanzo beans are the most widely consumed legume in the world.

Instant Bean Bonanza

Serves 6-8

Preparation time: 5 minutes

Simple, tasty, and high in protein and fiber, the hardest part about making this salad is opening the cans.

1	(15 oz.) can garbanzo beans		1	(15 oz.) can navy beans
1	(15 oz.) can kidney beans		1	(15 oz.) can green beans
1	small jar marinated artichoke hearts			your favorite vinaigrette

Drain and thoroughly rinse beans. Combine in large serving bowl. Pour marinated artichoke hearts, with or without liquid, over everything. Toss gently. Dress lightly with your favorite vinaigrette.

Bean Thread Salad

Serves 2-4

Preparation time: 30 minutes

This unusual salad is a feast for the eyes and the palate. The recipe sounds more difficult than it actually is. Experiment with a variety of vegetables, cut into various shapes and sizes. Bean thread is also called glass noodle or mung bean vermicelli and is available in any Asian market and most grocery stores. It requires no cooking.

10	oz. firm tofu (½ block)	1	cucumber, peeled and sliced
2	tsp. Bragg Liquid Aminos	1	c. watercress, chopped (optional)
1	(1.75 oz.) pkg. bean thread noodles	1	head romaine, cut into bite-size pieces
1	carrot, cut into matchsticks	1	small package clover sprouts
1	c. mung bean sprouts	6-8	cherry tomatoes (or other small tomatoes)
			sesame seeds for garnish

1. Wrap firm tofu (the kind packed in water) in cotton tea-towel. Let sit until towel is saturated. Unwrap and cut tofu into ¾-inch cubes. Drizzle lightly with Bragg Liquid Aminos.
2. Soak bean thread noodles in hot water for about 20 minutes or until softened.
3. Meanwhile, wash and prepare vegetables.
4. Drain softened noodles and toss with Cilantro-Sesame Pesto Dressing.
5. For each serving, place a layer of romaine on plate. Place about ¾ c. dressed noodles in center. Arrange vegetables in separate groups around noodles. Top with tofu cubes and clover sprouts. Garnish with cherry tomato halves. Sprinkle with sesame seeds. Eat with chopsticks—it's easier!

VARIATION: Cooked angel hair pasta, soba, or vermicelli may be substituted for bean thread.

Apple-Almond-Cranberry Salad

Serves 4-6

Preparation time: 5 minutes

Creamy and crunchy, sweet and tart, this nutritious, refreshing salad provides delightful contrasts of textures and tastes. Use the best quality organic yogurt (soy or dairy) available. Use all natural dried cranberries with few additives, such as Craisins by Ocean Spray, or Mariani brand.

2	celery stalks (with leaves), diced	⅓	c. almonds, slivered or sliced
2	apples, cored and diced	1	c. nonfat plain yogurt
⅓	c. dried cranberries or raisins	4	mints sprigs (optional garnish)

1. Toss all ingredients together in serving bowl.
2. Serve chilled in small bowls. Garnish with sprig of mint, if desired.

VARIATION: Pecans or walnuts may be substituted for almonds.

Indian Fruit Salad
with Spiced Tofu Dressing

Serves 8-10

Preparation time: 15 minutes   Chilling time: 30 minutes

Inspired by the exotic flavors and tropical fruits of India, this fabulous fruit salad is loaded with antioxidants. For best texture and appearance, serve within the hour. If making ahead, do not add bananas or dressing until moments before serving. For a beautiful 4th of July presentation, add starfruit (see next recipe).

2	c. strawberries, washed and sliced	2-3	bananas, peeled and sliced
2	ripe mangoes, peeled and diced	¼	c. blueberries or other berries
1	small, sweet pineapple, peeled, cored, and diced	1	Tbsp. fresh mint leaves (torn or whole)

1. Place strawberries in attractive serving bowl.
2. Add mangoes, bananas, and pineapple. (If pineapple is large, use only 1½ c. instead of the whole thing.)
3. For interest and color, toss in handful of fresh blueberries. Toss gently to combine fruits.
4. Cover bowl with plastic cling wrap and refrigerate for about 30 minutes.
5. Before serving, drizzle Spiced Tofu Dressing over fruit and toss gently. Sprinkle with fresh mint leaves.

Spiced Tofu Dressing

Yields ¾ cup

Preparation time: less than 5 minutes

This light, creamy, low-fat dressing is perfect for fruit salads, cabbage slaws, and simple leafy greens.

¼	c. pineapple juice	½	tsp. fresh ginger root, peeled and grated
2	Tbsp. honey or agave nectar	1	(12.3 oz.) pkg. Mori-Nu silken Lite tofu (soft is best)
1	tsp. vanilla extract	½	tsp. cinnamon

Combine all ingredients in blender and blend until very smooth, about 15 seconds. Store in small jar or bottle with tight-fitting lid. This keeps for about 1 week in refrigerator. Shake well before using.

Fourth of July Fruit Salad

Preparation time: 20 minutes

Chilling time: 30 minutes

The red, white, and blue combined with stars create a patriotic-themed all-American salad.

1	Indian Fruit Salad recipe	2	starfruit (carambola), sliced
1	Spiced Tofu Dressing recipe		blueberries, blackberries and/or strawberries for garnish

1. Follow the Indian Fruit Salad recipe and make the Spiced Tofu Dressing, but do not add dressing yet.
2. Slice starfruit (carambola) crosswise into "stars" and add to fruit mixture. Cover with plastic cling wrap and refrigerate for at least 30 minutes.
3. Before serving, layer the plain fruit mixture in transparent wine goblets, with scoops of Spiced Tofu Dressing between layers and on top (like a parfait). Garnish with blueberries and/or strawberry slices.

HINT: For a crowd, double or triple the recipe and layer ingredients and dressing in large transparent trifle bowl or punchbowl. For a patriotic effect, alternate layers of sliced strawberries and blueberries/blackberries between each layer of dressing. Top with a scattering of blue and red berries and a few starfruit slices.

Sauces, Spreads, and Snacks

Sauces and spreads dress up the most humble foods. Instead of the usual butter-based sauces and sour cream and mayonnaise-based dips and dressings, the following recipes rely on fresh and roasted vegetables, seasoned beans, healthy oils, and generous amounts of fresh herbs. Thicker dips can be scooped with crudités or organic chips, or spread on bread or rice cakes as a sandwich filling or butter replacement. Thinner sauces are ideal for drizzling on cooked vegetables and grains. Many of these spreads, dips, and sauces are essential elements in the snack recipes in this book.

Golden Sauce

Yield: 1¼ cups

Preparation time: 5 minutes or less

This creamy, versatile dressing is the ideal sauce for corn on the cob or baked potatoes, or as a topping for steamed vegetables, grains, casseroles, or salads. The flaxseed oil is an excellent source of Omega-3 fatty acids, the miso provides protein, and nutritional yeast flakes (available in bulk at health food stores) provide B vitamins, which are frequently lacking in vegetarian diets. The appearance, texture, and flavor satisfy cravings for something "buttery."

½	c. flaxseed oil (Barlean's is best)	1	Tbsp. nutritional yeast flakes
¼	c. apple cider vinegar	1	tsp. honey
2	garlic cloves	1	tsp. Dijon mustard
3	Tbsp. water	1	Tbsp. white miso (mellow)
		¼	tsp. salt

1. Combine everything in blender (or use hand-held immersion blender) and blend until smooth.
2. Pour into salad dressing bottle or small jar with tight-fitting lid. Keep refrigerated for up to 2 weeks. Shake well before using. (Note: This dressing thickens when chilled but thins out a bit at room temperature. A little more water may be added, if necessary. If using primarily for salads, increase water to at least ⅓ c.)

ABOUT NUTRITIONAL YEAST

An essential ingredient in certain recipes, nutritional yeast is rich in B vitamins, particularly B_{12}. Available in the bulk section of most health food stores, nutritional yeast is not used for baking or brewing. It is not a leavening agent. Do not confuse it with brewer's yeast! Nutritional yeast is an entirely different product and there is no substitute. Although it may seem expensive, a small amount goes a long way. Because nutritional yeast is very lightweight and is sold by the pound, you will only buy a few ounces at a time so the cost is minimal. It has a pleasantly cheesy flavor.

Herbs are not just garnishes or flavor enhancers. Packed with nutrients, herbs offer an array of health benefits such as invigorating circulation, relieving stress, aiding digestion, easing nausea, promoting restful sleep, and improving respiration. Many common herbs also have anti-viral, anti-fungal, and antiseptic properties.

Herb Pesto (Master Recipe)

Yield: 2-3 cups

Preparation time: 10 minutes

When your garden is overflowing, or you are inundated with herbs and greens, make a batch of pesto and freeze the extra for later. Toss with pasta and serve hot or at room temperature as a salad on a bed of romaine, garnished with brightly-colored vegetables. Feel free to experiment with various combinations and proportions of herbs and different kinds of nuts.

3-4	oil-packed sun-dried tomatoes (about 2 Tbsp.)	3	Tbsp. extra virgin olive oil
¾	c. pine nuts, toasted	3	Tbsp. nutritional yeast flakes
3-4	c. fresh basil, arugula, or parsley (or combination)	2-3	garlic cloves, peeled and mashed
		2	tsp. capers
		½	tsp. salt

1. Put everything in blender or food processor fitted with an S-blade. Process until mixture is about the consistency of thin peanut butter. A little more water will likely be required (add 1 Tbsp. water at a time until desired consistency is reached). If using blender, you may need to stop and start several times, scraping mixture down sides of blender before starting again. (Do not operate blender while scraping!)

2. Serve over hot pasta as an entrée or toss with pasta shells or corkscrews and cherry tomato halves and serve as salad on a bed of romaine. Pesto is also great on pizza and brown rice, and as a drizzle on creamy soups.

3. Left-over pesto should be stored in small airtight jar. Pour pesto in jar and drizzle lightly with olive oil to cover. Store for up to 1 week in refrigerator, or freeze immediately and thaw as needed.

VARIATION: Instead of sun-dried tomatoes, use up to 1 c. roasted red bell peppers (with liquid) from a jar. Try toasted walnuts or almonds instead of pine nuts. Experiment with different kinds and combinations of herbs. For a slightly less pungent flavor, use parsley or cooked broccoli for at least half the total amount of herbs.

Black Bean Dip

Serves 6

Preparation time: 5 minutes

Low-fat, fast, and fabulous, this high-fiber, mineral-rich dip is perfect with crudités (raw veggies) or Lundberg's organic brown rice cakes.

1	(15 oz.) can black beans, drained (reserve liquid) or 2 c. cooked black beans
2-3	Tbsp. reserved liquid from beans
3	Tbsp. fresh lime juice
2	garlic cloves, minced

¼-½	tsp. cumin
2-3	Tbsp. fresh parsley or cilantro, finely chopped, (optional)
	salt and pepper

1. Combine first 5 ingredients in blender and process until smooth.
2. Salt and pepper to taste. Stir in fresh parsley or cilantro just before serving.

White Bean Dip

Serves 6

Preparation time: 5 minutes

Follow recipe for Black Bean Dip, substituting navy beans (or other white beans such as Great Northern or lima). Omit cumin. Drizzle with extra virgin olive oil and garnish with parsley. Easy, tasty, and good for you!

HINT: Buy a small mortar and pestle to pulverize spices so you will always have fresh, aromatic spices as you need them. Pulverizing releases the flavor and aroma of cumin seeds and other spices.

Baba Ganouj (Middle Eastern Eggplant Dip)

Serves 6-8

Preparation and cooking time: 45 minutes

This fabulous dish isn't much to look at, but the intense, exotic flavors and creamy texture make it irresistible. Don't be intimidated by the roasting process—it's a snap to prepare! Measurements need not be exact and may be adjusted to suit individual tastes. Best served at room temperature with warm pita and veggies for dipping.

1 or 2 round eggplants (about 2 lb. total)	⅛ tsp. liquid smoke
1-2 Tbsp. tahini	1 ripe tomato (Roma preferred), diced
2-3 Tbsp. plain yogurt	1-2 Tbsp. parsley, chopped
juice of 1 or 2 lemons	salt and pepper

1. Preheat oven to 450 degrees. Lightly prick eggplant with fork. Use only firm, fresh eggplant. Place on parchment-lined baking sheet and roast about 30 minutes until charred. Outside should be almost burned and inside will be mushy. Remove from oven and let cool.
2. Meanwhile, combine tahini, yogurt, and lemon juice in bowl and mix with fork.
3. Remove skins from eggplant by slitting open and squishing out the flesh in bowl with other ingredients. Add liquid smoke. Mash everything with fork.
4. Fold tomato and parsley into creamy mixture. Salt and pepper to taste.
5. Serve as spread on crackers or brown rice cakes, filling for pita, dip for veggies and chips, or even as salad on a bed of romaine with red bell peppers and cucumber. Flavors intensify over time. Keeps 3 or 4 days in refrigerator.

ABOUT BAKING PARCHMENT

Parchment is a necessity in any kitchen, especially for the health-conscious cook. Available in a roll (like foil or waxed paper) it can be purchased at most supermarkets. It will save you from culinary disaster—you won't have burned or stuck-on food. Baking parchment makes for easy clean-up. A little-known fact about baking parchment: It can be washed (by hand) and reused, as long as no animal products (including eggs or dairy) have been in contact with the parchment. Parchment is essential in fat-free baking to prevent baked goods from sticking hopelessly to the pan. Foil is never a substitute for parchment.

Hummus (Middle Eastern Chickpea Appetizer/Dip)

Serves 6-8

Preparation time: 7 minutes

A lower-fat version of the classic Middle Eastern puréed chickpea (garbanzo bean) dish, this is made with canned beans to save time. High in protein, calcium, and fiber, hummus is best served as a dip for raw vegetables or spread on pita bread or brown rice cakes. As an appetizer, this recipe makes enough for a potluck or family. For one or two people, cut this recipe in half.

2	(15 oz.) cans garbanzo beans (or 3 c. cooked)	¼-⅓	c. lemon juice
2-3	Tbsp. tahini	½	tsp. salt (or less, to taste)
1-2	garlic cloves, peeled and mashed	1	Tbsp. extra virgin olive oil

1. Open cans of garbanzo beans. Use the kind with no sugar added (check label). Drain liquid into bowl. Reserve liquid.
2. Pour garbanzo beans into food processor or blender and add remaining ingredients.
3. Process until mixture is fairly smooth. Add some of the reserved liquid from the drained beans, a little at a time, until desired consistency is reached. A drizzle of extra virgin olive oil may be added. If using a blender, you will need to stop occasionally to push down chunks into blades with rubber spatula or wooden spoon. Repeat as necessary, stopping, pushing down, blending again. The longer it is blended, the smoother it gets. Adjust blending time and speed accordingly, to your preference. (Note: Hummus is kind of like peanut butter in texture. It can be thick and chunky, or smooth and creamy.)
4. Adjust seasonings to taste. For more intense flavor, add a little more lemon juice and salt.
5. Place hummus in an attractive shallow bowl. Drizzle with a little extra virgin olive oil. Serve at room temperature as dip for raw veggies, or spread on organic brown rice cakes and topped with cucumber and sprouts. Store tightly covered in refrigerator and use as soon as possible.

VARIATION: Reconstitute several sun-dried tomatoes in ⅔ c. hot water. When softened, add to blender and pulse several seconds. If a thinner texture is preferred, add a little of the soaking water before pulsing.

Garden Salsa

Yield: about 5 cups

Preparation time: 5 minutes

Garden-fresh flavors and brilliant colors characterize this simple, nutritious, versatile condiment.

3-4	ripe tomatoes (at least 2 c.), diced	2	large lemons or limes (about ¼-⅓ c. juice)
½	c. purple onion, diced	1	jalapeño pepper, seeded and finely chopped
½	c. cilantro, chopped (optional)		salt and pepper

1. Combine tomatoes, cilantro and onion in bowl. Use as many tomatoes as you wish.
2. Squeeze juice of fresh lime or lemon over everything. Add jalapeño (omit if you prefer mild salsa). Season with salt and pepper to taste.
3. Serve with tortilla chips or as a condiment for Mexican dishes of all kinds. This salsa is best served fresh, but will keep several days if refrigerated. Flavors intensify with time.

Avocado Dip (Guacamole)

Serves 6-8

Preparation time: about 5 minutes

The success of this dip depends on the ripeness of the avocados. Use only perfectly ripe (not over-ripe), non-stringy avocados with no dark spots.

2-3	avocados	¼-½	tsp. garlic salt (a few shakes, to taste)
1	Tbsp. fresh lime juice (or lemon juice)	1	Tbsp. cilantro, minced (optional)
	dash Tabasco, sriracha or other hot chili sauce		

1. Slice avocados in half, lengthwise. Remove pit (save it) and scoop avocado flesh into bowl of food processor fitted with an S-blade. (Or use bowl and fork to mash the avocado.)
2. Add remaining ingredients and process (or mash) until mixture is almost smooth but still a bit chunky.
3. Spread on brown rice cakes or use as dip for vegetables or tortilla chips. Place avocado pit in bowl with remaining dip to keep dip from turning brown right away. Use within 24 hours.

> Avocados, once cut, should be used immediately or rubbed with lemon juice or lime juice on the cut surface to prevent discoloration. Avocados are a good source of Vitamins E and C, iron, potassium, and manganese and are beneficial to the skin and hair. Spread ripe avocado on whole grain bread or rice crackers instead of butter. Yummy!

Raita (Indian Yogurt Condiment)

Serves 6

Preparation time: 5 minutes

This refreshing condiment is essential to all curry dishes, and is adaptable as a dip for veggies and fruits. Use the best quality yogurt available (no gelatin or corn starch added).

1½	c. plain yogurt	1	tsp. ground cumin (or use pulverized cumin seeds)
1	cucumber, finely diced		salt
½	tsp. ginger root, peeled and grated		pinch of cayenne pepper

1. Combine yogurt, cucumber and ginger in medium bowl.
2. Toast cumin in dry pan for about 1 minute until fragrant. Do not burn. Add to yogurt mixture. Sprinkle lightly with salt and gently mix.
3. Dust with cayenne pepper just before serving. Serve chilled as dressing, dip, or condiment for vegetables, grains, chips, and salads. If your family or guests eat meat, fish or poultry, Raita is a refreshingly light condiment for this heavier fare. Raita will keep for 3 or 4 days in refrigerator.

ABOUT YOGURT

Good-quality yogurt contains live bacteria cultures. Even people who are lactose intolerant can usually enjoy dairy yogurt because the lactase produced by these live bacteria cultures digests the yogurt lactose. Soy yogurts are available for vegans and others who do not eat dairy products, but the flavor is slightly sweet and the color is not pure white. Avoid yogurts with added fruit, sweeteners, corn starch, gelatin, or chemicals. Organic yogurt is best. Do not buy yogurt that is made from milk produced by cows that have been given antibiotics or growth hormones (rBGH/BST). Yogurt and cheese made with milk from goats and sheep generally are more pure than products made from cow's milk, because most goats and sheep are not treated with antibiotics or growth hormones. Carefully read all ingredient labels, especially on low-fat or nonfat yogurt, as many brands add corn starch and gelatin to give the yogurt more body. Greek-style yogurt is very thick and rich, high in calories but perfect for tzatziki.

Tzatziki
(Middle Eastern Yogurt-Dill Sauce)

Serves 8

Preparation time: 2 to 4 hours draining time, plus 5 minutes to make

This simple delicious sauce is the perfect accompaniment to couscous, quinoa, salads, pilaf, dolmades (stuffed grape leaves), and stuffed pita sandwiches. It is also a delectable dip for vegetables, naan, pita, and chips. Tzatziki can be made with a nonfat yogurt IF you use only the best quality gelatin-free yogurt (check label) that has no added corn starch, or it will not thicken. If available, use the best quality thick Greek yogurt and skip the straining.

1	qt. plain yogurt (the kind with no gelatin)	1	Tbsp. fresh mint, minced
½	medium cucumber, diced into ¼-inch cubes	1-2	tsp. fresh lemon juice
1	garlic clove, peeled and minced	1	tsp. extra virgin olive oil
2	tsp. fresh dill weed (or ½ tsp. dried dill weed)	¼	tsp. salt (or more to taste)

1. Line strainer with cone-shaped coffee filter and place over deep bowl. Scoop yogurt into filter and let drain several hours in refrigerator. Yogurt thickens as it drains. Allow yogurt to drain until desired consistency is achieved (2 to 4 hours). Remove yogurt from filter by inverting it over another bowl and peeling away the filter. Or just use good, thick Greek-style yogurt and you can skip this draining process.
2. Add cucumber to bowl with thickened yogurt. Add all remaining ingredients. Stir gently.
3. Enjoy immediately as dressing, dip, or sauce. Store remainder in tight-sealed container. Flavors intensify over time, so beware of garlic!

VARIATION: For a taste surprise, replace lemon juice with fresh lime juice.

Instead Spread

Yield: 2 cups

Preparation time: 1 minute

Use instead of mayonnaise to spread on bread for sandwiches or to bind sandwich fillings. Instead Spread is creamy, tangy, and entirely fat-free!

2	c. plain yogurt
¼	c. Dijon mustard

1. Mix good-quality yogurt with Dijon mustard. If thicker product is desired, use Yogurt "Cream Cheese" instead of plain yogurt.
2. Use as needed. Store in tightly sealed jar. This should keep at least a week in refrigerator.

Yogurt "Cream Cheese"

1 quart yogurt = 2 cups "cheese"

Drain time: 4 hours or overnight

Preparation time: 5 minutes

Make yogurt "cream cheese" ahead of time and keep refrigerated. Use only plain gelatin-free yogurt. Most nonfat yogurts contain gelatin and other additives; yogurts with gelatin will not thicken when drained.) Yogurt cream cheese can be substituted for regular cream cheese in most recipes. This recipe has only 1 ingredient!

PLAIN YOGURT (gelatin-free)

1. Line strainer with cone-shaped coffee filter and place over deep bowl. Scoop good-quality dairy yogurt into filter and let drain about 4 hours in refrigerator. The longer it drains, the thicker it gets.
2. When desired consistency is achieved, remove yogurt from filter by inverting it over a bowl and peeling away the filter.
3. Use like cream cheese, or create your own blends (see Goat Cheese Schmears for inspiration).

Gomasio (Gomashio)

Yield: about ½ cup

Preparation time: 10 minutes

High in iron, calcium, and Vitamins A and B, Gomasio can be sprinkled over beans, grains, vegetables, soups, and stews. Dulse and kombu are sea vegetables (seaweed/kelp) found in Japanese markets and the Asian section of most supermarkets. The dried sea vegetables keep for years if stored in a dark, dry place.

½	c. hulled sesame seeds
1	oz. dulse or kombu
½	tsp. salt

1. Dry-roast sesame seeds in skillet over medium heat for about 3 minutes, stirring frequently, until they have a nutty aroma and begin to pop. Dry-toast dulse or kombu in skillet until crispy.
2. Combine everything in blender or food grinder. Add salt. Pulse until most seeds are crushed and dulse or kombu is almost powdery.
3. Sprinkle on popcorn, rice, salads, vegetables, and other foods. Store remainder in glass jar with tight lid.

Gremolata

Yield: about 1 cup

Preparation time: 5 minutes

Resting time: 30 minutes

Aromatic, intense, and easy to make, gremolata is a feast for the senses. This flavorful, beautiful, healthful garnish can be sprinkled on salads, vegetables (steamed, roasted, or marinated), sandwiches, grains, fish, and countless other savory dishes. Allow at least 30 minutes for flavors to marry.

zest of 1 lemon
1   bunch parsley (up to 1 c.), minced
1   garlic clove, minced

Fluff lemon zest, parsley and garlic together. Let sit for at least 30 minutes before using. Refrigerate and use within 24 hours.

VARIATION: For an entirely different taste sensation, substitute any other leafy herb for all or part of the parsley. Cilantro or basil are good choices, if you like the flavor.

Goat Cheese Schmears

Preparation time: 2 minutes or less

Fresh goat cheese (chèvre) can be used like cream cheese. Tone down the strong flavor of goat cheese by adding a little extra virgin olive oil. Spread over bagels, pita, brown rice cakes, or crackers, or use as a dip for fresh veggies or chips. The sweet schmears are great as a dip for sliced apples and pears. For an easy appetizer, make several kinds of schmears (multiply the recipes to accommodate the number of guests) and serve with a variety of crackers, rice cakes, crudités, fruits, and garnishes. Your guests will have fun creating their own appetizers. Here are some ideas, each designed for individual portions:

PLAIN: Mash together ¼ c. fresh goat cheese with up to 1 tsp. extra virgin olive oil.

DILL: Add ½ tsp. fresh dill weed (or more, to taste) to plain schmear (above).

GARDEN: Add 1 tsp. diced celery, 1 tsp. shredded carrot, and 1 tsp. fresh parsley to plain schmear.

CHIVE: Add ½ tsp. snipped chives to plain schmear.

PESTO: Add ½ tsp. fresh minced basil, 1 clove minced garlic, 1 tsp. finely chopped pine nuts and 1 more tsp. extra virgin olive oil to plain schmear.

PINK: Add a little juice from cooking beets. Mix together and enjoy the lively color and hint of sweetness.

BASIL & SUN-DRIED TOMATO: Chop 2 tsp. sun-dried tomatoes, 1 tsp. fresh basil, and 2 Kalamata olives and add to plain schmear.

APRICOT-WALNUT: Finely chop 1 Tbsp. dried apricots and 2 tsp. walnuts, and add to plain schmear.

CINNAMON-RAISIN: Add 1 Tbsp. chopped raisins, a generous sprinkle of cinnamon and a dab of honey to plain schmear.

PINEAPPLE: Add 1 Tbsp. crushed pineapple to plain schmear.

Tomato-Tofu Relish

Serves 8

Preparation time: 10 minutes, if tofu has been pre-drained and "squeezed"

This simple, no-cook relish works equally well as a dip or spread with crusty bread, tossed with pasta and served hot as an entrée, served at room temperature as a salad, or as a topping for baked potatoes. It also makes an excellent topping for Instant Pizza. This is a potluck favorite with chunks of fresh sourdough bread. Flavor intensifies with time. Keeps up to 4 days, if refrigerated.

8-10	oz. firm tofu (packed in water)	2	Tbsp. balsamic or red wine vinegar
1	(14.5 oz.) can diced tomatoes	¼	c. extra virgin olive oil
10-15	Kalamata olives, pitted and chopped	¼	tsp. salt
2	garlic cloves, minced	3	Tbsp. basil, chiffonaded
1	Tbsp. chopped purple onion (optional)		ground black pepper to taste

1. Cut tofu in half. Wrap ½ block (8 to 10 oz.) in cotton tea-towel and let sit until towel is thoroughly saturated. Place the remaining tofu in tightly sealed container, covered with cold water. Refrigerate for later use.
2. Place strainer over deep bowl. Pour tomatoes into strainer. Set aside. Save liquid for soup or stock.
3. Crumble prepared tofu into separate bowl. Add olives, garlic, and onion to bowl.
4. Add balsamic or red wine vinegar, olive oil, and salt to tofu mixture. Mix with fork and marinate 5 minutes.
5. Add drained tomatoes to tofu mixture. Top with coarsely ground black pepper. Adjust seasonings and add more olive oil or reserved liquid from tomatoes, if desired. Mix again with fork. Add fresh basil just before serving. Stir gently to mix.

TOFU BASICS

Tofu is one of the most versatile, nutritious foods on the planet. Almost everyone can enjoy the benefits of tofu, a marvelous source of protein, calcium, and phytoestrogens. Unfortunately, very few people know how to prepare it, and without proper care and preparation it is an almost tasteless, quivering, watery white mass. Therefore, READ THIS and follow the instructions carefully BEFORE YOU BEGIN ANY RECIPE THAT CALLS FOR TOFU!!! It will make all the difference.

RULE #1. BUY ONLY ORGANIC OR NON-GMO TOFU. Because tofu is made from soybeans, most of which are genetically modified (potentially dangerous!), stick to brands that specifically indicate the product is made from organic or non-GMO soybeans.

RULE #2. USE THE RIGHT KIND OF TOFU FOR THE RECIPE. Tofu comes in many forms, consistencies, and types. If you use the wrong kind for the recipe, it will be like using parmesan cheese instead of cream cheese—the recipe won't turn out right. Several companies sell tofu that has been marinated and baked, available in a variety of flavors for immediate use (no draining necessary). The main kinds of tofu used in this cookbook are:

Japanese silken tofu: Packaged in aseptic boxes (10 oz. or 12.3 oz sizes), with a shelf life of about 12 months, silken tofu is available in soft, firm, and extra firm. Mori-Nu makes a "Lite" tofu. Used mainly in desserts, creamy and custard-like dishes such as pies and quiches, it acts as a substitute for eggs and dairy products in many recipes. Silken tofu should not be used in meat-like dishes unless it has been frozen and thawed, as it is too slippery and the texture is unsuitable.

Water-packed fresh tofu: Packaged in water and found in the refrigerator section, this tofu comes in various sizes (usually 14, 16, and 20 oz.) and degrees of firmness (soft, firm, extra-firm). It is extremely perishable. Once opened, the water must be replaced daily or the tofu will spoil. Use within 7 days. Firm or extra-firm is recommended for most dishes. Used mainly in stir-fry and meat-like dishes, this tofu readily absorbs the flavors around it. In order to absorb these flavors, tofu must first be drained and the excess moisture removed. Here's how:

RULE #3. DRAIN AND WRAP WATER-PACKED TOFU BEFORE USING IN RECIPE. Drain and rinse tofu. Fold a non-terry-cloth dishtowel in half, lengthwise. DO NOT USE A TOWEL THAT HAS BEEN WASHED IN FABRIC SOFTENER OR MACHINE-DRIED WITH SCENTED DRYER SHEETS. Place tofu across the end of the towel, wrap and tightly roll up in towel. Let sit until the towel is thoroughly saturated. If you prefer a denser cake of tofu, wrap and roll again in another towel. An easy method is to double-wrap in 2 towels and let sit in the refrigerator overnight, or for at least 2 hours. Now the tofu is ready for the recipe. (Note: All Chinese-style tofu requires this preparation.)

RULE #4. CHANGE WATER DAILY IF NOT USING TOFU ALL AT ONCE. If you don't, the tofu will spoil rapidly. Cover tofu with water and keep refrigerated until ready to use. Drain and wrap tofu according to Rule #3, then proceed with the recipe.

RULE #5. FREEZE TOFU ONLY IF RECIPE INDICATES. Freezing drastically affects the texture and characteristics of tofu. Unless specifically stated in a recipe, do not use tofu that has ever been frozen or the recipe will not turn out as intended. However, certain recipes actually call for tofu that has been frozen and thawed. Frozen tofu that has been thawed and drained has a "meaty," chewy texture. Tofu that has been frozen for several hours or overnight has a texture similar to a fish filet. Tofu that has been frozen for several days develops a more chicken-like texture.

HOW TO FREEZE TOFU: Cut block of tofu into strips, cubes, or slices, according to the recipe. Any kind of firm or extra-firm tofu (water-packed or silken) can be successfully frozen. Place on a baking tray and cover with plastic cling wrap. Layer the tofu and cover each layer with cling wrap. Cover and freeze overnight or longer, depending on desired texture (the longer the better). To thaw frozen tofu, remove from the freezer and let sit at room temperature for 1 hour. Drain and pat dry with a towel.

Lentil Spread

Serves 6

Preparation and cooking time: 30 minutes

Delicious as a spread for Lundberg's brown rice cakes or as a dip for vegetables, this humble spread provides extra protein and fiber. It can be made chunky or smooth, depending on how long it is blended.

⅔	c. lentils (the brownish-green kind)		up to ¼ c. lemon juice
3½	c. water	1	tsp. plus 2 tsp. extra virgin olive oil
1	small onion, minced (about ½ c.)	½	tsp. salt
3-4	garlic cloves, minced		fresh herbs or other garnish

1. Bring water to rolling boil. Slowly sprinkle in lentils while water keeps boiling. Cover and reduce heat to medium. Cook for about 25 minutes, or until most of water is absorbed and lentils are chewy-soft.

2. Meanwhile, heat 1 tsp. extra virgin olive oil in small frying pan. Add onions and garlic, reduce heat and sauté 2 to 3 minutes or until onions are translucent. Stir frequently and do not allow to burn!

3. Combine sautéed onions and garlic with cooked lentils. Stir in salt, lemon juice, and 2 tsp. extra virgin olive oil.

4. Dump everything into food processor or blender. Process until desired creaminess (or chunkiness) is achieved. You may have to scrape down sides of blender with spatula, stopping and starting a few times. Add more olive oil or lemon juice if you wish (but it's perfect as is, in my opinion).

5. Serve at room temperature as dip for vegetables or spread for brown rice cakes. Garnish with something colorful (fresh basil, parsley, purple onion rings, grated carrot) to enhance this plain-looking dip.

VARIATION: Make Lentil Sauce by adding 2 c. water when preparing above recipe. Adjust seasonings to taste. Great over brown rice or other cooked whole grains, as well as steamed vegetables.

Tahini-Garlic Sauce

Yield: 3 cups

Preparation time: less than 4 minutes

A delicious, creamy sauce suitable for grains, vegetables, or Tofu-Spinach Balls.

1 c. tahini	2 Tbsp. Bragg Liquid Aminos
1 c. plus 1 c. very warm water	½-⅔ c. fresh lemon juice (do not substitute!)
2 tsp. garlic (3-4 cloves), minced	¾ c. cooked rice

1. Combine tahini, 1 c. water, garlic, Bragg Liquid Aminos, and lemon juice in saucepan. Stir over low heat.
2. In blender, combine cooked rice and 1 c. very warm water. Put the lid on tight. Blend at high speed until completely smooth. Add to sauce in pan and bring to boil. Reduce heat to simmer.
3. Pour hot Tahini-Garlic Sauce over Tofu-Spinach Balls, or serve as gravy over veggie burgers or cooked whole grains.

Summer Rolls with Hoisin-Peanut Sauce

Preparation time: varies, depending on how many you make and what you put in them

Beautiful, refreshing, light, nutritious, tasty, and a great way to use up whatever is lurking in the vegetable crisper, these colorful Vietnamese-inspired appetizers are simple to prepare and make a grand impression.

1 pkg. rice wrappers	1 red bell pepper, seeded and cut into strips
1 bunch leafy lettuce	mung bean sprouts (a large handful)
1 cucumber, cut into narrow wedges	1 avocado, peeled and sliced
1 carrot, cut into matchsticks (or use pickled carrot and daikon, available at some Asian Markets)	fresh mint or basil (leaves from several sprigs)
	fresh chives, separated into single blades

1. Prepare and arrange in assembly line fashion.
2. Prepare very smooth, large, flat surface to work on. Fill large bowl with very warm (not hot) water.
3. Remove 1 rice paper wrapper. Submerge in warm water and remove immediately. It will continue to soften. Shake off excess water and lay wrapper on flat work surface.
4. Carefully lay lettuce leaf on lower half of 1 wrapper. Layer small amount of prepared veggies in a strip across, just below the center. Layer veggies as much as possible.
5. Roll wrapper like a burrito, folding in ends as you roll. Just before you finish rolling, place single blade of chive across the wrapper, with both chive ends sticking out about 2 inches. Finish rolling. Seal edge with moistened fingertips and place edge down on serving platter. Repeat process until all veggies are used up, or you run out of rice wrappers, or you don't want to make any more.

6. To serve, cut summer rolls in half diagonally. Arrange artfully on platter with Hoisin-Peanut Sauce in small bowl in the center. (Note: Summer rolls are best if made fresh, as wrapper tends to toughen within an hour. If making summer rolls in advance, cover with damp tea-towel and then with plastic cling wrap. Keep refrigerated until serving.)

Hoisin-Peanut Sauce

Yield: ⅔ cup

Preparation time: 2 minutes

Perfect for dipping summer rolls and other Asian appetizers, this flavorful dip is almost instant. Buy hoisin sauce in a bottle in most supermarkets or any Asian market.

⅓   c. hoisin sauce

⅓   c. water

1-2   Tbsp. chunky peanut butter (any kind)

Stir together ingredients in small saucepan over medium heat. When well mixed, remove from heat. Serve warm or cold.

Brown Rice-Cake Open-Face Sandwiches Serves any number

Preparation time: 5-10 minutes

Lundberg's organic or nutra-farmed brown rice cakes form the foundation of these hearty snacks. Use only brown rice cakes, not the Styrofoam white rice cakes. The possibilities are endless, depending only on your imagination and the toppings available.

BASE:	Lundberg's Brown Rice Cakes (any flavor)	
SPREADS (choose one):	Lentil Spread	Black Bean Dip
	Hummus	Avocado Dip (Guacamole)
	White Bean Dip	Fresh Goat Cheese Schmear
	Tahini (sesame seed butter)	Peanut Butter
	Almond Butter	Tofu Scramble
	Chickpea Sandwich Spread	Mock Egg Salad

ENHANCEMENTS:

alfalfa or clover sprouts	pumpkin seeds
sunflower seeds	fresh herbs
cucumber slices	olives
raisins	banana slices
onion rings	steamed or roasted veggies
tomato slice	lettuce (shredded or
dried cranberries	whole leaf)

1. Spread brown rice cakes with your choice of spread.
2. Top each with an assortment of any suggested enhancements, according to your own taste.

Soybeans in the Pod (Edamame)

Serves 4-6

Preparation time: 1 minute

Cooking time: 15 minutes

A fun, delicious, messy way to eat soybeans! Buy the frozen soybeans in pod (called Edamame), available in the freezer section of most supermarkets. Use fresh ginger root and garlic. Edamame is an excellent source of protein. Even kids love them!

1 (16 oz.) bag frozen edamame	5	garlic cloves
2-inch piece of ginger root	1	Tbsp. Bragg Liquid Aminos

1. Put edamame in colander or sieve and rinse with hot running tap water.
2. Fill large pot about ⅓ full of edamame. Cover with water.
3. Smash garlic cloves with flat side of knife blade. Thinly slice ginger. Add ginger and garlic to pot.
4. Drizzle Bragg Liquid Aminos over everything. Bring to boil. Lower heat and simmer for about 10 minutes or until soybeans are slightly tender. (Test them.)
5. When cool enough to eat, pop the pod into your mouth and suck out the beans. Discard the pod. Alternate method: Open pod with fingers and eat the beans.
6. Store remainder, with liquid, in glass jar with tight-fitting lid. This keeps well for up to 5 days if refrigerated. ONLY USE CLEAN FORK or other clean utensil to retrieve soybeans from jar. Bacteria from fingers (no matter how "clean") cause faster spoilage.

Nori Burritos

Serves any number, 1 person per nori sheet

Preparation time: 5 minutes, if spread or dip is already made

Nori works well as a wrapper for sandwich fillings and is an excellent source of iron and other minerals. This recipe is very adaptable—kind of a tasty catch-all for bits of leftovers. Be creative with your choice of spreads and toppings. For variety and added nutrition, try different kinds of sprouts such as broccoli, clover, alfalfa, radish, or whatever you can find. Enjoy!

1. Lay out 1 sheet of nori (sushi seaweed) per person and spread thinly with your choice of spreads or dips from this book. Leave ½-inch margin around edges. Here are some suggested spreads and other toppings:

    Goat Cheese Schmear with watercress, cucumber spears, sprouts, grated carrot

    Goat Cheese Schmear with roast veggies, fresh basil

    Avocado Dip with sprouts, fresh basil or cilantro, sunflower seeds, lettuce

    Lentil Spread with sprouts, fresh thyme/oregano/basil, cucumber spears, pumpkin seeds

    Black Bean Dip with grated carrot, avocado slice, cucumber spears, cilantro, sprouts

    White Bean Dip with fresh basil, cucumber spears, grated carrot, parsley, sunflower seeds

    Hummus with cucumber spears, grated carrot, sprouts, parsley

    Almond Butter with grated carrot, cucumber spears, sprouts, dried cranberries

2. Top with your choice of toppings. Roll up like a burrito. Moisten inside edge of nori and press edges together to secure. Place seam side down on plate. Eat whole or cut in half.

Veggie Wraps

Serves any number

Preparation time: varies, depending on choice and number of ingredients

These wraps are a fun way to use up leftovers and fresh veggies. Do not overfill the tortilla or it will be difficult to wrap and even more difficult to eat. One wrap per person should satisfy even the heartiest appetite! Here is a recipe for a single wrap.

BASE: 1 large flour tortilla per person
             (any kind—try spinach or sun-dried tomato for a change)

SPREAD (choose ONE of the following):

Hummus	Guacamole	Schmears
Pesto	Black Bean Dip	other favorite healthy spread
Lentil Spread	White Bean Dip	

FILLINGS:

¼   c. cooked brown rice
½   tsp. Bragg Liquid Aminos
½   c. beans or leftover cooked vegetables (optional)
¾   c. greens (lettuce, cabbage, spinach, sprouts, fresh herbs, your choice)
any healthy salad dressing (your choice)

1. Spread tortilla with ONE spread, making sure to cover the entire surface.
2. Place rice in strip across diameter of tortilla. Drizzle lightly with Bragg Liquid Aminos.
3. Arrange any leftover cooked vegetables or beans next to rice across diameter of tortilla.
4. Scatter greens over tortilla. Lightly drizzle with any dressing from this cookbook or any healthy dressing.
5. Roll up tortilla like a burrito, tucking in both sides over filling when rolling it up.
6. Wrap snugly in foil or plastic wrap. Stand it upright in large mug to serve. Peel back foil or plastic as you eat.

Trail Mix

Preparation time: 2 minutes

An excellent source of Vitamin E, calcium, B vitamins, fiber, and protein, this healthful snack should be enjoyed in moderation because of its high fat and sugar content. Great for quick energy on the go!

1. Mix together an assortment of your favorite raw, shelled nuts and seeds, and dried fruits. Use any amount of any ingredient, as long as you include things from each category (Nuts, Seeds, Dried Fruits). Here are some ideas:

   NUTS: walnuts, almonds, Brazil nuts, cashews, pecans

   SEEDS: sunflower seeds, pumpkin seeds (pepitas)

   DRIED FRUITS: raisins, dates, prunes, goji berries, banana chips, dried cranberries, mango

2. Place the trail mix in Ziploc plastic bag or glass jar with tight lid and store leftovers in refrigerator or freezer. Better yet, divide into snack-size portions in snack-size Ziploc plastic bags.

SECRETS TO PERFECT POPCORN EVERY TIME

Secret #1: Buy the cheapest plain popcorn you can find (health food store bulk section or store brand), put it in a Ziploc freezer bag and store it in the freezer. Freezing popcorn keeps the moisture content of each kernel high and even, which makes the kernels pop evenly when heated, leaving fewer unpopped kernels.

Secret #2: Season popped corn immediately (while still steamy) with powdered salt (see p. 62). Powdered salt tends to adhere to anything. It tastes saltier, so you will use less.

Secret #3: If cooking popcorn on the stovetop, cover the bottom of a stainless steel pot or skillet with thin layer of canola oil. Turn heat on high. When the oil starts to get hot, test temperature by putting a single kernel (yes, only one) into the pot with the hot oil. When tiny bubbles form near the kernel of popcorn, add 2 tablespoons of popcorn kernels to the hot oil, place a lid snugly over the pot, and listen to the magic happen.

Secret #4: When popping slows down (about 2-second intervals between pops), remove pot from stove but leave the lid on for 1 more minute to avoid surprise eruptions of any as-yet-unpopped kernels. Serve in a large bowl and season with powdered sea salt.

Fat-Free Microwave Popcorn   Serves 2

Preparation and cooking time: less than 3 minutes

Although I am not a fan of microwave ovens or microwaved food, this method offers a fat-free way to indulge in popcorn. This popcorn costs almost nothing to make and tastes great!

2   Tbsp. popcorn kernels   Powdered Salt (see below)

1. Scoop popcorn into paper bag (lunch bag size). Twist top tightly (about 2 inches from top of bag). Wet paper bag under running water.
2. Put bag in microwave and microwave on High for about 2 minutes, listening carefully. (Amount of time depends on brand of microwave.) When popping slows down (intervals of 2 seconds between pops) remove bag from microwave.
3. Carefully untwist top of bag, with the opening facing away from you to avoid steam burns. (Do not leave bag in microwave too long or popcorn will burn and smoke will fill bag and ruin the whole batch.) Sprinkle liberally with powdered salt and enjoy!

How To Make Powdered Salt

Pour 2 c. sea salt, Hawaiian salt, or kosher salt in blender. With lid on tight, process on high speed for a few seconds until "cloud" of powder floats out when lid is removed. Pour powdered salt into small jar with tightly sealed lid and use for seasoning popcorn, baked chips, or anything that regular salt does not adhere to. For some reason, this powdered salt has the ability to stick to food instead of falling to the bottom of the bowl.

PIZZA PARTY IDEA

This kind of party is perfect for "mixed" groups—vegans, carnivores, kids, teens, dieters, heart patients, diabetics, etc. Have each guest bring their favorite pizza topping ingredient and their favorite beverage to share. Set up pizza ingredients (see next 2 recipes) buffet-style and have guests create their own pizzas. Pop pizzas in the oven or stovetop or even on the grill (with a cover). These pizzas brown quickly, so delegate a guest or 2 to keep an eye on them while they are cooking. Use any leftover toppings to make a salad or antipasto platter. This party satisfies everyone and is easy on the cook. Bravo!

Instant Personal Pizza

Serves 1

Preparation time: 10 minutes

Baking time: 15 minutes

As versatile as your imagination, instant pizzas can be assembled in minutes using prepared crusts, sauce, and assorted vegetables. Use pita or naan (Indian flatbread) for the crust, and a good quality bottled pasta sauce (low-fat, sugar-free; Classico brand Tomato and Basil pasta sauce is an excellent choice) as a base. This works equally well as a cheese-less pizza, believe it or not!

BASE:	naan or pita
SAUCE:	pizza sauce, pasta sauce (in jar), or pesto
TOPPINGS, your choices:	tomatoes, sliced (fresh or sun-dried)

TOPPINGS, your choices:
- tomatoes, sliced (fresh or sun-dried)
- onion, sliced thin
- Tomato-Tofu Relish
- mozzarella or almond mozzarella
- oregano or Italian seasoning blend
- artichoke hearts, quartered
- baby spinach
- mushrooms (fresh or canned), sliced thin
- bell peppers (all colors), sliced or diced
- zucchini, sliced thin
- olives (all kinds), sliced or chopped
- fresh basil, thyme, marjoram or oregano (optional)

1. Preheat oven to 375 degrees.
2. Place pita or naan directly on oven rack and pre-bake for 2 minutes. Assemble and chop/slice an assortment of toppings.
3. Remove warmed pita or naan from oven and place on parchment-lined baking sheet or pizza pan. Smear evenly with pasta sauce or pesto. (Hint: If making only 1 or 2 pizzas, use stovetop method below.)
4. Top with your choice of prepared toppings. If desired, sprinkle with a little grated mozzarella or almond mozzarella. (Note: Almond mozzarella is the only nondairy mozzarella that actually melts and doesn't get rubbery. Do not use soy "mozzarella," it will ruin pizza.) Sprinkle with fresh basil or dried oregano. Bake in preheated oven for about 15 minutes or until it looks "done." Be careful not to let pizza dry out in oven.

VARIATIONS: Omit mozzarella entirely. Top with Tomato-Tofu Relish and veggies instead. If topping with spinach, add a few crumbles of feta. This pizza actually tastes fabulous without any cheese!

Stovetop Pizza (thin-crust)

Serves 1-2

Preparation and cooking time: 5-10 minutes, depending on toppings

Ideal for one or two people, this simple stovetop method creates a perfect crisp crust while leaving the toppings fresh and succulent. The toppings are the same, but the crust is a flour tortilla. Use the largest tortilla that will fit your skillet.

1. Assemble and prepare your choice of toppings (see previous recipe for suggestions).
2. Put large flour tortilla in skillet. Turn heat to medium-low.
3. Spread even layer of pasta sauce or pesto over entire tortilla. Work quickly.
4. Arrange toppings on pizza. Work quickly; pizza is cooking.
5. Place lid on skillet. Turn heat off.
6. Keep lid on while pizza continues cooking until bottom of crust is golden brown but not black, and toppings are hot and gooey. Leafy toppings such as spinach should be wilted and cheesy topping should be melted.

Stuffed Veggies Unlimited

Serves any number

Preparation time: 5-10 minutes, if spread is already made

This recipe is truly "unlimited" because you are not limited to any particular filling or combinations. You are not even limited to using celery! Try "stuffing" hearts of romaine, cucumber "boats," zucchini, or anything else. A great way to use up leftover bits from last night's dinner. Important: To avoid molds and other things that aggravate good health, all leftovers should be consumed or frozen within 24 hours.

1. Wash and trim vegetable(s) to be stuffed. Choose from:

| celery stalks | zucchini boats | hearts of romaine |
| endive | cucumber boats | radicchio leaves |

2. Stuff with any of the following:

Black Bean Dip	Lentil Spread	Mock Egg Salad
White Bean Dip	Hummus	Goat Cheese Schmear
Almond Butter	Avocado Dip	Peanut Butter

3. As a fancy appetizer, arrange on a bed of dark leafy greens on serving tray and garnish with carrot curls, radish roses, and parsley. For everyday quick snacking, just grab and munch.

Roll-Ups

1 roll-up serves 2 people as an appetizer

Preparation time: 10 minutes

Resting time: 2 hours or overnight

Similar to Veggie Wraps, this variation makes an attractive appetizer or light lunch. It is also a great way to use up bits of leftovers. Roll-ups can be as individual as the person creating them. No two have to be alike. Just use whatever ingredients you have on hand, and enjoy the outcome!

Thin-Thins (flexible rectangular thin tortilla-like unleavened flatbread)
spread of choice (see Veggie Wrap recipe for ideas)
beans or leftover cooked vegetables (optional)
greens (lettuce, cabbage, spinach, sprouts, fresh herbs, your choice)
bell pepper strips
avocado slices
cucumber wedges

1. Spread Thin-Thin with your choice of spread. Leave a 1-inch margin at top and bottom. Scatter greens and optional fillings thinly and evenly over entire surface.
2. Place strips of bell pepper, avocado slices, cucumber wedges, or whatever you like across bottom end.
3. Roll up snugly and wrap tightly in plastic wrap. Refrigerate until ready to serve. To serve, cut into 1-inch wheels with serrated knife. Arrange on platter and serve as an appetizer.

Sesame-Tofu Nuggets

Serves 2-4

Preparation time: 10 minutes, if tofu has been pre-drained

Baking time: 30 minutes

A perfect accompaniment to Asian stir-fries or served on their own dipped in plum sauce, sesame-tofu nuggets provide an excellent source of protein and calcium.

1   (16 or 20 oz.) block firm or extra-firm tofu   dark sesame oil
Bragg Liquid Aminos   sesame seeds

1. Drain tofu. Cut in half and wrap each half in double layer of cotton tea-towel. Let sit until towel is thoroughly saturated, at least 20 minutes. Preheat oven to 350 degrees.
2. Slice tofu blocks in half horizontally, then vertically into strips (total 16 to 20 strips). Spread in single layer on plate. Very lightly drizzle tofu strips with Bragg Liquid Aminos and sesame oil.
3. Roll each tofu strip in sesame seeds (instead of nutritional yeast mixture) and place close together on parchment-lined baking sheet. Put in oven and bake for about 30 minutes. Serve with plum sauce for dipping, if desired.

Tofu Mock Chicken Nuggets

Serves 2-4

Preparation time: 10 minutes, if tofu has been pre-drained

Baking time: 30 minutes

A great way to introduce tofu to skeptics, these nuggets can be eaten with fingers. Because they are baked instead of fried, the fat content is low and no hovering is required. Be sure to use baking parchment (not foil!) to prevent sticking and to expedite cleanup. Enjoy plain or serve with ketchup, hoisin-peanut sauce, barbecue sauce, or your favorite dipping sauce and pretend you are eating "junk food."

1	(16 or 20 oz.) block extra-firm tofu	¾	c. nutritional yeast flakes
	Bragg Liquid Aminos	¼	tsp. garlic salt
	extra virgin olive oil	½	tsp. oregano or Italian herb blend

1. Drain tofu. Cut in half and wrap each half in double layer of cotton tea-towel. Let sit until towel is thoroughly saturated, at least 20 minutes. Preheat oven to 350 degrees.
2. Slice tofu blocks in half horizontally, then vertically into strips (total 16 to 20 strips). Spread in single layer on plate. Very lightly drizzle tofu strips with Bragg Liquid Aminos and olive oil.
3. On another plate, use fork to mix together nutritional yeast flakes, garlic salt and dried oregano or Italian herb blend. Roll each tofu strip in mixture, using tongs. Shake off excess, place close together (but not touching) on parchment-lined baking sheet. (Note: Extra yeast mixture may be stored in small jar or airtight container for future use.)
4. Bake for about 30 minutes or until slightly golden brown.

ABOUT BRAGG LIQUID AMINOS

This all-purpose seasoning is pure vegetable protein made only from soybeans and purified water. Although the flavor is somewhat similar to a mild soy sauce or tamari, it is not fermented and contains no alcohol, wheat, additives, chemicals, preservatives, or coloring agents. Bragg Liquid Aminos is Kosher certified. Even people with allergic sensitivity to soy or wheat may use Bragg Liquid Aminos. Unlike soy sauce, Bragg Liquid Aminos does not overpower dishes in which it is used.

Soups and Sides

Soups and side dishes don't have to stay on the sidelines. Easy enough for everyday cooking, many of these recipes may become regular features or even entrées on your menu. Because legumes, vegetables, and grains form the basis of many soups and sides, they are perfect "one pot meals." Combined with a fresh green salad and brown rice cakes or whole grain bread, they make a wholesome, filling lunch or light dinner.

Soup is nourishing, hearty, and comforting. There are no "rules" about making soup, and most recipes are infinitely adaptable. Remember that grains and legumes expand, so don't add more than the recipe calls for or you may end up with a gooey blob instead of soup. Make extra and freeze for later (see note at end of Lentil-Barley Soup recipe). To freshen soup that has been frozen and then thawed, add a handful of chopped greens or herbs during last few minutes of reheating. Experiment with variations and enjoy the adventure!

Quick Cream of Vegetable Soup

Serves 4

Preparation and cooking time: 5-10 minutes

This recipe uses "fresh" leftovers from a previous meal. Results are as varied as your imagination and the ingredients you have on hand. The creamy texture comes from the cooked rice and blended ingredients.

1	onion, chopped	½	c. cooked brown rice (short grain makes a creamier soup)
1	tsp. extra virgin olive oil		
2	c. cooked vegetables	2	c. water or vegetable broth
			salt and pepper

1. Sauté onion in olive oil over medium heat. Add leftover cooked vegetables (broccoli, cauliflower, carrots, zucchini, peas, green beans are good choices), cooked brown rice, and water or vegetable broth. Heat until warm but do not boil.
2. Pour half the soup in blender. Holding lid on tightly, blend until creamy smooth. Repeat process with remaining soup.
3. Reheat blended mixture in pot, season to taste with salt and pepper. Serve with garnish of choice.

Silky Bean Soup

Serves 2

Preparation and cooking time: 10 minutes

Almost instant, this soothing soup relies on canned beans and fresh herbs. Great Northern or navy beans may be substituted for pinto beans.

2	(15 oz.) cans pinto beans , undrained	2	c. water or vegetable broth
¼	c. onion, chopped		salt and pepper
2	garlic cloves, peeled and minced		fresh herbs (optional)
1	tsp. oregano		toasted nuts (optional)

1. Open cans of beans and dump into medium pot, or use 3 to 4 c. cooked beans. Add onion, garlic, oregano, and water or vegetable broth. Cover and cook 5 minutes.
2. Pour soup into blender. Cover lid with small towel. Hold blender lid on tight. Blend until very smooth. (Alternate method: Use handheld immersion blender and blend soup in pot. With this method, soup may not be as creamy.)
3. Salt and pepper to taste. Garnish with chives, cilantro, or other fresh herbs. Top with toasted nuts.

HOW TO COOK (ALMOST) FART-FREE BEANS

A lot of mythology surrounds the cooking of beans. These basic guidelines will demystify bean cooking and alleviate gas problems to a great extent. To summarize: Soak beans overnight, change the water, bring beans to a boil, scoop off all foam, and use a pressure cooker (in spite of what the manufacturers tell you). Here's how:

1. Buy the biggest, best pressure cooker available.

2. Buy dry beans in bulk, if possible. Sort through the beans to remove small rocks and debris before soaking.

3. Scoop beans into a mixing bowl, filling the bowl only about ¼ to ⅓ full. Cover beans with cool water to at least 3 inches above the beans to allow them to expand as water is absorbed. Soak beans overnight. NEVER skip this process or try to hurry it. This applies to all beans except black-eyed peas, split peas, mung beans, and lentils.

4. Drain soaked beans in a colander and rinse well. Dump beans into a pressure cooker. Add fresh water to at least 3 inches above beans. Do NOT put lid on. Do NOT add salt or any seasoning.

5. Bring pot to a rolling boil, keeping an eye on it. Beans will begin to foam and froth. With a large long-handled ladle, gently scoop off all foam and froth. Lower heat to medium. Continue scooping off until all foam is removed. By this time you will probably have a bowl full of foamy liquid. Throw out this foamy liquid. Add a 2-inch strip of kombu (dried kelp—see glossary) to the pot to reduce gas.

6. Place lid securely on pressure cooker and seal well, according to directions in the manual. Turn heat on high. When pressure has built up you will hear a very loud sound of steam being released. This is exactly what is supposed to happen. Ignore the noise for 3 minutes (5 minutes if cooking garbanzo beans).

7. After 3 minutes (or 5 minutes for garbanzos), turn heat off but do not remove pressure cooker from stove. When noise stops, let sit for at least 10 minutes (or up to 30 minutes if you wish), then gradually turn valve on lid to release pressure—or you can remove the pot from the stove and run cold water over it. Remove lid, add salt according to taste, and use in any recipe that calls for this type of bean.

8. When cool, scoop remaining beans into jars with tight-sealing lid. Allow at least 1½ inches of head room if storing in a freezer. Food expands when frozen, and an over-filled jar will crack and break in the freezer. Alternately, freeze in any airtight container. Even plastic containers can crack in the freezer, and any warm food will expand when frozen. Cooked beans are great to have on hand for quick soups, Mexican dishes, hummus and other dips and spreads, casseroles, salads, etc.

(Note: Home-cooked beans may turn out a little softer and not as "pretty" as those from a can, but in my opinion the flavor is far superior to canned beans.)

Yellow Mung Beans with Purple Onion   Serves 2-3

Preparation time: 30 minutes

Tasty, easy, and attractive, this dish provides plenty of protein and fiber.

5 c. water	pepper (few grinds)
¾ c. hulled split dried yellow mung beans	2 tsp. plus 1 Tbsp. extra virgin olive oil
1 tsp. salt (to taste)	1 purple onion, coarsely chopped
¼ tsp. ground cumin (optional)	

1. Bring water to rolling boil. Sprinkle in split dried yellow mung beans. Continue boiling, skimming off any white foam (this step reduces gas, so don't skip it!). When beans become soft, stir in cumin, salt, pepper, and 2 tsp. olive oil. For creamier beans, blend with immersion hand blender before serving.
2. In small frying pan over medium heat, sauté purple onion in 1 Tbsp. olive oil, until translucent (do not burn!). Serve cooked beans in individual serving bowls topped with sautéed onions. Wow!

Barley Soup   Serves 8+

Preparation and cooking time: 1 hour

This hearty, savory soup is simple to make and adapts well to most vegetables. It thickens with time, so if any is left over more liquid may be required. Make a large batch and freeze in family-size portions. Serve with crusty whole grain bread or Irish Soda Bread and a crispy green salad.

2 c. water	2 c. V8 or tomato juice
1 medium carrot, coined or diced	½ c. pearl barley
2 c. cabbage, shredded	1 (15 oz.) can diced tomatoes
2 celery stalks (with leaves), chopped	salt and pepper
1 small zucchini, diced	3 garlic cloves, peeled and minced
¼ c. onion, chopped	Bragg Liquid Aminos
¾ c. corn (fresh, canned, or frozen)	

1. Put everything in large pot. Bring to boil, reduce heat, cover, and simmer for 45 minutes.
2. Adjust seasoning. Add generous squirt of Bragg Liquid Aminos, if desired.

Basic Bean Soup

Serves 4-6

Preparation and cooking time: 10-15 minutes

This soup relies on canned beans and finely diced fresh vegetables as well as any leftover vegetables or grains from a previous meal. Use your imagination! If you don't like something, leave it out. If you like something, add it to the pot. If you have the time and inclination, cook your own beans from scratch and substitute canned beans with home-cooked beans.

½	onion, chopped	1	(15 oz.) can diced tomatoes with liquid (optional)
1	celery stalk (with leaves), chopped		
2-3	garlic cloves, minced	¾	c. cooked brown rice or pearl barley (OR ⅓ c. uncooked)
1	c. zucchini and/or carrot , chopped		
3-4	c. cooked beans (2 cans)		leftover cooked vegetables, any amount (optional)
1	Tbsp. Bragg Liquid Aminos		
2	c. water or vegetable broth	1	Tbsp. extra virgin olive oil
1	c. greens (spinach, chard, kale, cabbage, or whatever is on hand)	1	tsp. liquid smoke (optional)
		2	tsp. lemon juice
			salt and pepper to taste

1. Heat olive oil in medium pot and sauté onion, celery, garlic, zucchini, and carrot for about 2 minutes or until onion is soft.

2. Drain and rinse canned beans to remove excess salt and sugar. Use any kind of bean—navy, pinto, black, Great Northern, kidney, garbanzo, etc.—in any combination.

3. Add beans to pot. Add water and Bragg Liquid Aminos (or use vegetable broth, if available). Add tomatoes with liquid.

4. Add rice or pearl barley. If you're not in a hurry and can wait 45 minutes for grain to cook in the soup, add uncooked brown rice or pearl barley instead.

5. Add any cooked vegetables or other savory goodies from the previous meal (optional).

6. Chop greens. If using cabbage, add to pot at least 10 minutes before serving. All other greens should be added just before serving to retain bright color. Season with salt and pepper. Just before serving, add lemon juice to pot. For smoky "ham" flavor and aroma, add liquid smoke and stir well.

7. Garnish with your choice of garnishes. (See Garnishes for Soups and Sides.)

Lentil-Barley Soup

Serves 4

Preparation and cooking time: 1 hour

Simply delicious, this satisfying soup provides complex carbohydrates and protein for a steady supply of energy. A meal in itself!

2	tsp. extra virgin olive oil	1	carrot, diced
4	garlic cloves, peeled and mashed	1	tsp. oregano
½	onion, chopped	2-3	Tbsp. lemon juice
1	celery stalk (with leaves), diced	5	c. water
½-1	tsp. salt (to taste)	¼	c. pearl barley
1	c. brown lentils	1	c. greens (spinach, chard, etc.), chopped
	pepper		

1. In large pot over medium heat, sauté garlic, onion, and celery in olive oil for 2 minutes.
2. Add water, lentils, carrot and barley to pot. Bring soup to boil, cover, lower heat and simmer 50 minutes.
3. When lentils and barley are soft, add remaining ingredients. Use immersion hand blender to purée part of soup in pot if you prefer a fairly creamy texture.
4. If desired, stir in greens just before serving.

HOW TO COOK LENTILS, MUNG BEANS, AND SPLIT PEAS

No need to pre-soak or pressure cook! This works for all types of lentils, mung beans, split peas, and even black-eyed peas. The secret is in the method:

1. Bring a large pot of water to a rolling boil. Use at least 3 cups of water for every 1 cup of lentils/peas.

2. Meanwhile, sort through lentils to remove small stones and debris.

3. While water continues to boil, gradually sprinkle in lentils a little at a time so the water continues to boil rapidly and lentils keep circulating. Continue boiling, scooping out any foam or froth that forms on top. Boil furiously for at least 10 minutes.

4. Reduce heat to low. Cover with a lid and cook another 10 minutes. Lentils are done when soft and tender.

5. When done, season to taste. NEVER add salt until lentils are soft, as salt reduces the lentils' ability to absorb liquid and they will take much longer to cook. Use cooked lentils as they are, or in recipes.

Split Pea-Barley Soup

Serves 4

Preparation and cooking time: about 75 minutes

A variation of Lentil-Barley Soup, this creamy soup lends itself to experimentation with different vegetables and seasonings. The kombu (kelp) is optional but enriches the mineral content and flavor of the soup.

1	Tbsp. extra virgin olive oil	1	carrot, diced
1	onion, minced	1	parsnip, diced (optional)
1	stalk celery (with leaves), diced	1	small zucchini, diced
6	c. water	1	tsp. salt (or more, to taste)
1	c. dried split peas		pepper
¼	c. pearl barley		fresh herbs (optional)
	4-inch strip kombu (dried kelp)	½	tsp. liquid smoke

1. In large pot over medium heat, sauté onion and celery in olive oil for 2 minutes.
2. Add water, peas, barley and kombu to pot and bring to boil. Reduce heat, cover and simmer for 45 minutes.
3. Add carrot, zucchini, and parsnip to pot. Cover and simmer 15 minutes or until peas and barley are soft and vegetables are tender.
4. Season with salt, a few grinds of black pepper, and a handful of fresh herbs such as oregano, basil, or thyme. For smoky aroma and flavor, add liquid smoke at the very end of cooking. Stir well. (Note: Split peas and barley expand and thicken with time. Unless eaten immediately, you will definitely have to add more water when soup is reheated!)

VARIATION: Soup thickens even more when chilled, so serve this as dip or spread the next day. Freeze the rest.

HOW TO FREEZE SOUP

If there is any soup left over, cool it down and freeze in an airtight container. Freeze it in quantities that you are most likely to use (e.g. 1, 2, or 4 servings) because once soup has thawed it should not be refrozen. Do not freeze soup that has potato in it. Fill container ¾ full, allowing plenty of space for expansion (at least 2 to 3 inches). Soup expands as it freezes, and container will crack if filled too full. I learned this the hard way and had to throw out a jar of delicious soup because of the broken glass.

Creamy Polenta with Sun-Dried Tomatoes

Serves 4

Preparation and cooking time: 5-10 minutes

The secret to this creamy, simple, satisfying dish is the method. The coarse cornmeal (polenta) must be sprinkled in gradually while the water continues boiling rapidly. If the water stops boiling, this indicates that the polenta is being added too quickly, so slow down! Otherwise it will get lumpy.

3½	c. boiling water	1	Tbsp. nutritional yeast flakes
3	sun-dried tomatoes (dry, not from jar)	¼	c. corn kernels (fresh, canned, or frozen)
½	tsp. salt	¼	tsp. red chili pepper flakes
1	c. coarse cornmeal (polenta-style)	¼	c. grated almond cheese, any flavor (optional)

1. Bring water to boil. Snip or cut sun-dried tomatoes into small bits. Add salt and sun-dried tomato bits to boiling water.
2. While water continues to boil, gradually sprinkle cornmeal into boiling water, stirring continuously with wire whisk. Do NOT "dump" cornmeal into water or it will lump!
3. Add nutritional yeast. Continue stirring to avoid lumps. Cook about 3 minutes, until mixture begins to thicken.
4. Add corn, chili pepper flakes, and almond cheese if you like. Stir well and serve immediately. Mixture continues to thicken as it sits, so a little more water may be added, if necessary.
5. A light drizzle of extra virgin olive oil may be stirred in just before serving, if desired. Any leftover polenta may be pressed ½-inch thick into an oil-coated baking pan and baked at 350 degrees for a few minutes, until golden brown. Cut baked polenta into squares or triangles and top with spread of your choice for a unique appetizer.

GARNISHES FOR SOUPS AND SIDES

Fresh herbs: parsley, basil, cilantro, scallions, oregano, dill, chives, celery leaves, or any compatible herbs. Include herbs that have gone into the soup itself. Chop or use sprigs to garnish.

Fresh greens: spinach, arugula, leafy lettuce, or mesclun. Finely slice or chiffonade and sprinkle on top of soup just before serving. They wilt and turn bright green!

Toasted seeds or nuts: toast raw, shelled seeds, or nuts. Float like croutons on top of soup. Pumpkin and sunflower seeds, slivered almonds, or walnut pieces are good choices, adding texture and protein to creamy soups.

Sauces: a spoonful of cilantro-sesame pesto, ginger-lime-dill dressing, or any dressing from this book will add sparkle and perk up a bland soup, salad, grain, or vegetable dish.

Lemon or lime: fork a lemon or lime and let the juice drizzle into the soup or side dish to enhance flavors.

Extra virgin olive oil: drizzle a dab of good extra virgin olive oil on the surface of hot soup. The heat brings out the full aroma of the oil. Good olive oil is the perfect "finishing oil" for many dishes; add a few drops just before serving.

Freshly-cracked black pepper: use a pepper mill set on coarse grind.

Toasted seaweed: toast nori, dulse, or kombu in a dry skillet until crispy. Sprinkle crisp bits of toasted seaweed over soups, salads, grains, and veggie dishes to boost flavor and mineral content.

Gremolata: made with garlic, parsley, and lemon, gremolata enhances almost any savory food.

Gomasio: a sprinkle garnish made of sesame seeds and seaweed, gomasio fortifies with minerals, vitamins, and flavor.

Grains: press cooked rice or barley into a decorative mold (or use ½ cup measure). Unmold into bowl and ladle soup over it. Serve immediately and impress your guests.

Sprouts: clover, broccoli, alfalfa, sunflower, lentil, and various other sprouts add a colorful, nutritious touch to many soups.

Salts: alaea salt, Celtic sea salt, or other specialty salts with herbs add a nice finishing touch.

Gazpacho

Serves 4-6

Preparation time: 20-30 minutes

Chilling time: 4 hours

This beautiful, refreshing chilled soup is ideal for hot summer days when fresh vegetables are abundant and tomatoes are perfectly ripe.

4	yellow or red bell peppers, seeded and diced		4	large ripe tomatoes, cored and diced
2	Japanese cucumbers, peeled and coarsely chopped		2	c. V8 or tomato juice
			⅓	c. balsamic vinegar or red wine vinegar
2	cloves garlic, peeled and minced		1	Tbsp. capers
				salt and pepper

Just before serving:

¼   c. purple onion, finely diced

6   parsley sprigs

1   avocado, diced

1. Place above ingredients EXCEPT onion, parsley, and avocado in large bowl. Stir well.
2. Place half mixture in blender or food processor. Purée slightly.
3. Return purée to bowl. Shortly before serving, add onion. Important: Do not add onion until just before serving or it will overpower the bright, delicate flavors of the other ingredients.
4. Salt and pepper to taste. Mix with spoon.
5. Cover tightly and refrigerate about 4 hours to allow flavors to marry. Serve in chilled individual bowls (transparent bowls add a nice touch) and garnish with fresh parsley and/or diced avocado.

Pineapple Gazpacho

Serves 4-6

Preparation time: 20 minutes

Chilling time: 1 hour

A simple chilled soup with a tropical twist, this gazpacho features fresh pineapple instead of tomatoes. It's an excellent source of vitamins and a delicious, painless way to eat fruits and vegetables.

1	small fresh pineapple (low-acid if available)		2	Tbsp. lemon or lime juice
1	red bell pepper, seeded and chopped		2	c. pineapple juice
1	yellow bell pepper, seeded and chopped			dash Tabasco (optional)
1	Japanese cucumber, peeled and diced			salt (alaea preferred)
1	small bunch parsley, chopped			parsley sprigs or diced red bell pepper for garnish

1. Peel and core pineapple. Cut into bite-size chunks. Retain as much juice as possible.
2. Toss everything EXCEPT pineapple juice into blender. Purée until almost smooth. Add pineapple juice. For thinner consistency, add a bit more juice. Salt to taste. To kick it up a notch, add a dash of Tabasco sauce.
3. Pour into bowl. Cover tightly and refrigerate at least 1 hour. This soup is best served the same day.
4. Garnish with a sprig of parsley or diced red bell peppers.

Spinach with Black-eyed Peas   Serves 4

Preparation and cooking time: 10 minutes, if using canned black-eyed peas

This hearty dish may be served warm or at room temperature.

1	lb. fresh spinach or chard (about 6 c.)	⅔	c. black-eyed peas, drained and rinsed
1	large onion, coarsely chopped	salt	
1-2	Tbsp. extra virgin olive oil	pepper	

1. If using chard, remove leafy part from stem by holding leaf upside down by the stem, then stripping the leafy part from each side of stem with your other hand. Tear chard leaves and dice stems.
2. In large skillet over medium heat, sauté onion (and chard stems if using chard) in 1 Tbsp. olive oil until translucent. Add spinach or chard leaves. Stir constantly for about 1 minute, or until greens start to wilt but are still bright green. (Note: Frozen chopped spinach, fully thawed and squeezed "dry," may be substituted for fresh. Use 1, 8 oz. package.)
3. Add beans to pot. Stir. Season with salt and pepper to taste.
4. Drizzle a little more extra virgin olive oil just before serving. Toss gently. Cool to room temperature if serving as salad, or serve warm as a side dish.

HINT: Black-eyed peas require no pre-soaking and are very quick to cook from scratch. If you want to cook your own, here's how: Cover ⅔ c. dry black-eyed peas with water in small pot. Bring to boil. Simmer until tender, about 30 minutes. Check for doneness. Do not overcook or they will turn mushy. Add salt at the end of cooking time.

Butternut-Ginger Soup

Serves 4

Preparation and cooking time: 15 minutes

Creamy, satisfying, and high in beta-carotene, this soup makes a great lunch or an attractive first course.

½   butternut squash
2   Tbsp. extra virgin olive oil
1   medium white or yellow onion, chopped
5   garlic cloves, peeled and chopped
2-inch piece ginger root, peeled and thinly sliced

1   tsp. mushroom seasoning (optional, but well worth it!)
sea salt (omit if using mushroom seasoning), to taste
parsley, cilantro, or pumpkin seeds for garnish

80

1. Cut 1 butternut squash in half, lengthwise. Remove seeds. Place cut side down in skillet. Add water to ½-inch level. Put lid on and bring water to boil. When it starts to boil, turn heat to low. Simmer until squash is tender. Remove squash from skillet.

2. Heat olive oil in medium-size pot over medium heat. Add chopped onion, garlic, and ginger and sauté 2 minutes. Stir constantly to avoid scorching.

3. Scoop out flesh of squash and put in pot with onions, garlic, and ginger. Add water from steaming the squash. Reduce heat, cover, and simmer for 5 minutes. If soup is too thick, add more water. Adjust seasoning. For added depth of flavor, add mushroom seasoning (available in Asian markets).

4. Pour about ⅓ of soup into blender. Cover lid with small towel. Hold blender lid tightly. Blend until creamy smooth. Dump blended soup into another pot. Repeat process with remaining soup until all soup is smooth. WARNING: This soup is like molten lava, so hold blender lid on very tightly to avoid an eruption!

5. Garnish with a sprig of cilantro or parsley or float several raw pumpkin seeds on top, if you wish.

Potato Potage

Serves 4-6

Preparation and cooking time: 35 minutes

This delicious, hearty, creamy soup is completely dairy-free. It soothes the soul, nourishes the body, and is easy to prepare.

2-3	large potatoes (3 c.), peeled and diced	1	Tbsp. Bragg Liquid Aminos
1	small white or yellow onion (about ⅔ c.), diced	2	c. plain soymilk or Almond Milk salt and pepper
3	c. water	2	Tbsp. nutritional yeast flakes
1	tsp. lemon juice	1	c. leafy greens (spinach, arugula, mustard greens, or kale), chopped
½	tsp. dried dill weed (or 1 tsp. fresh dill)		

1. Combine potatoes, onion, water, and lemon juice in medium pot. Bring to boil.

2. Add dill weed and Bragg Liquid Aminos. Reduce heat, cover, and simmer for about 15 minutes until potatoes are tender.

3. Purée soup with immersion blender, leaving some chunks, if desired. Add soymilk. Salt and pepper to taste.

4. Stir in nutritional yeast flakes. Add greens to pot. Cook about 2 minutes or until greens are tender and bright green (time depends on type of greens).

5. Add more soymilk or water if soup is too thick. Adjust seasoning, if needed. Serve with whole grain bread and fresh garden salad.

Grains & Garlic

Serves 4-6

Preparation time: 2 minutes

Cooking time: 50-60 minutes

Aromatic, simple, and delicious, this can easily be prepared in an automatic rice cooker or a large pot. Vary the proportions and combinations of grains and the amount of garlic according to personal preference and availability of ingredients. Basically, this is a three-ingredient dish: grain, garlic, and olive oil.

2	c. brown rice (or other whole grains, any combination)		
3½	c. water	1	whole head of garlic (unpeeled)
½	tsp. salt		extra virgin olive oil

1. In rice cooker or large pot with lid, place brown rice, water, salt, and garlic. Do NOT divide garlic head into separate cloves.
2. Drizzle a little extra virgin olive oil over everything. Cover pot, bring everything to boil, and reduce heat to simmer. Cook 50 minutes or until water is absorbed and rice is chewable.
3. Before serving, drizzle a little more olive oil and toss gently. Remove garlic, squish out the creamy "guts," and mix into rice or add to hummus or lentil spread. Sprinkle with Gremolata, if desired.

HINT: If you have any left over, use within 24 hours as the basis for Rice Tabouli, Rice and Pea Salad, Multi-Grain Zucchini Salad, or any other grain-based dish.

Sesame Rice with Petite Peas

Serves 4-6

Preparation time: 1 minute

Cooking time: 50 minutes

This variation on the previous recipe is enhanced by sweet, tender, baby peas, providing a burst of color and texture contrast. Be sure to add the peas immediately before serving, or they will turn a strange, unattractive color.

2	c. brown rice (long or medium grain)	2	tsp. dark sesame oil
3½	c. water	⅔	c. frozen petite peas
½	tsp. salt		Gomasio or toasted sesame seeds

1. Combine rice, water, and salt in rice cooker or large pot with lid. Cover and bring to boil. Reduce heat and simmer about 45 minutes or until water is absorbed and rice is tender but not mushy.
2. At very end of cooking time, add peas and sesame oil. Toss gently. Serve as soon as possible so that peas retain their bright green color. Garnish with a generous sprinkle of Gomasio or toasted sesame seeds.

A single rice seed can yield more than 3,000 grains of rice.

Fast Asparagus

Serves 6-8

Preparation and cooking time: 5 minutes

Asparagus is an excellent source of folate, boron, Vitamin E, and glutathione. Here's a simple, quick way to enjoy it. Choose young, slender stalks (pencil-thin, if possible) and eat your fill!

1	lb. asparagus	½	lemon
1	Tbsp. extra virgin olive oil		salt to taste

Asparagus spears can grow up to ten inches in one day.

1. Snap woody ends off slender asparagus stalks. Allow about 2 oz. per person. Wash well.
2. Diagonally slice asparagus stalks into 1½-inch pieces.
3. Heat olive oil in skillet over medium heat. Add asparagus pieces and stir-fry 3 to 4 minutes. Asparagus will turn bright green. For crisp-tender stalks, cook less time. For more well-done stalks, cook a bit longer.
4. Season with salt and squeeze juice from half a lemon over asparagus at end of cooking time. Toss gently and serve immediately. (Asparagus turns brownish if it cooks too long or sits around awhile.)

Baked Dilled Asparagus

Serves any number

Preparation time: 5 minutes or less

Cooking time: 10-15 minutes

This "no-brainer" is a snap to make and is perfect with any baked entrée. Bake at same temperature as whatever else is in the oven, or wrap loosely in foil and bake in a toaster oven if making only enough for one or two people.

asparagus

fresh dill

Bragg Liquid Aminos

1. Wash, snap off woody ends, and place whole asparagus stalks in baking dish. If asparagus stalks are thick, cut in half horizontally before baking. If making only a small portion, place asparagus, Bragg Liquid Aminos and dill in foil instead of baking dish, then wrap up with the edges firmly sealed on top.
2. Pour water over asparagus (about ½-inch deep). Squirt Bragg Liquid Aminos lightly over everything (about ½ tsp. per serving). Lightly sprinkle with fresh dill (up to ½ tsp. per serving).
3. Place uncovered in hot oven (350 degrees or whatever temperature oven is set at). Bake for 10 to 15 minutes or until done to desired tenderness. Do not overcook or will be mushy. Be careful when opening oven to remove asparagus, as steam is very hot.
4. Serve immediately, or place in covered serving dish. (Asparagus gets cold very quickly.)

HINT: Use pencil-thin asparagus if available. Thick stalks will need to be peeled with vegetable peeler or cut in half horizontally, or they will be disgustingly tough and stringy.

Quick Cabbage Oriental

Serves 6

Preparation and cooking time: 10-15 minutes

An Asian variation of the previous dish, this flexible recipe features thinly julienned vegetables and a hint of Oriental flavor. Use the freshest seasonal vegetables in whatever quantities and combinations you like.

1 head green cabbage or Chinese Napa cabbage (won bok)	1 tsp. Bragg Liquid Aminos (or to taste)
1 Tbsp. extra virgin olive oil or sesame oil	½-1 tsp. dark sesame oil
½-inch ginger root, peeled and chopped	salt
2 garlic cloves, peeled and chopped	pepper
1 pkg. chop suey vegetable mix	1-2 Tbsp. toasted sesame seeds

1. Finely shred cabbage. A mandolin or food processor makes quick work of this job.
2. Heat olive oil in bottom of deep skillet. Sauté ginger and garlic for about 1 minute. Add shredded cabbage, cover, and let steam for 3 to 4 minutes.
3. Uncover, add chop suey vegetable mix and Bragg Liquid Aminos. Stir-fry 2 minutes or until chop suey mix is heated through.
4. Drizzle with sesame oil. Salt and pepper to taste. Sprinkle with toasted sesame seeds (see below).

VARIATION: Add whatever cruciferous vegetables you have available. Broccoli and cauliflower, cut into tiny "trees," are tasty and attractive choices.

HINT: Food cooks faster and flavors meld better when the ingredients are cut small and shredded fine. This makes a huge difference, so do it! Proper cutting and shredding take only moments, and food cooks much faster so nutrients and flavor are retained. You'll save a lot of time in the long run by putting forth a little extra effort initially.

Baby Bok Choy

Serves 4-6

Preparation and cooking time: 15 minutes

These perfect little vegetables are beautiful, delicious, tender, and nutritious.

4	baby bok choy	1-2	tsp. dark sesame oil
½	tsp. salt	1	tsp. Bragg Liquid Aminos

1. Cut baby bok choy in half, lengthwise, allowing 1 per person. Soak in water for 10 minutes to remove dirt. Rinse well. Pay careful attention to base of stem, where dirt hides.
2. Put about ½ inch water in large skillet. Bring to simmer and add salt. Place bok choy (cut sides down) in simmering water. Cover and cook about 3 to 4 minutes, until bright green and tender.
3. Gently place on serving dish and drizzle lightly with dark sesame oil and/or Bragg Liquid Aminos.

Long Beans with Slivered Almonds

Serves 4-6

Preparation time: 2 minutes

Cooking time: 10 minutes

Long green beans found in Asian markets work best for this dish. They are not stringy and require no special preparation or trimming. Green Lake beans may be substituted. Almonds dress up the humble bean and add protein and calcium, and red bell pepper lends a festive touch.

6-8	oz. long beans, sliced into 2-inch pieces	⅓	c. slivered almonds
1	medium onion, diced	1	Tbsp. red bell pepper, diced
1	Tbsp. (or less) extra virgin olive oil		

1. Fill a large pot ⅔ full with water and bring to rolling boil.
2. Dump beans into boiling water and cook for about 2 minutes, or until bright green but still a little crisp.
3. In large skillet, heat olive oil. Sauté onion over medium-low heat until translucent. Add slivered almonds. Stir.
4. Drain beans and add to skillet. Stir-fry for 2 minutes or until beans are as tender as you like them but still bright green. Sprinkle with finely diced red bell pepper. Salt to taste.

VARIATIONS: Omit almonds and use pine nuts instead.

Herbed Snap Peas

Serves 4

Preparation and cooking time: 5 minutes

Enjoy the flavors of spring in this quick and easy dish. For variety and color, toss in a small carrot cut into matchsticks.

1	lb. snap peas	2	Tbsp. fresh dill, basil, or mint
1	small onion, chopped		salt
1	tsp. extra virgin olive oil		pepper

1. Fill skillet with enough water to barely cover bottom. Add peas and onion. Stir-fry together for 2 minutes.
2. Add olive oil and herbs. Salt and pepper to taste.

Greens with White Beans

Serves 2-4

Preparation and cooking time: 15 minutes

Rich in minerals, vitamins, and protein, this simple dish can be as varied as your imagination. Use your favorite dark leafy greens—kale, chard, collard greens, spinach, beet greens—and your favorite white bean, such as cannelloni, Navy, Great Northern, butter beans, or even black-eyed peas. Read the bean can label to check for added sugar (!!) and don't forget to drain and rinse canned beans to remove any added sweeteners.

2	bunches kale or other dark leafy greens	1	(15 oz.) can white beans or 2 c. cooked white beans
1	Tbsp. extra virgin olive oil		juice of 1 lemon
1	small onion, chopped		salt
2	garlic cloves, minced		pepper

1. Wash kale or other greens. Remove any tough stems and ribs. Chop or tear the leaves.
2. In large skillet or wok, sauté onion and garlic in olive oil for about 2 minutes or until onion is translucent.
3. Add wet chopped kale, stir-fry for 3 minutes or until greens are wilted and tender but still bright green. Drain and rinse beans. Add beans to skillet.
4. Heat through, add a bit more water if needed, salt and pepper to taste, and squeeze a little fresh lemon juice over everything (see How to Fork a Lemon).

Italian Vegetable Sauté

Serves any number

Preparation time: 5 minutes

Cooking time: 20 minutes (including oven time)

This brilliant, beautiful, aromatic side dish will delight your eyes and your taste buds. The secret is in the pre-roasting, which brings out the sweetness of the vegetables before they are sautéed. Make sure you use only the freshest vegetables available! Great over linguini.

mushrooms (including portabella)

bell peppers (red, yellow, orange)

zucchini (green and yellow)

purple onion

eggplant

extra virgin olive oil

salt

basil (fresh or dried)

1. Preheat oven to 425 degrees.
2. Cut equal amounts of mushrooms, bell peppers, zucchini, onion, and eggplant into bite-size chunks. Arrange in single layer on parchment-lined baking sheet.
3. Roast in oven for 10 minutes until vegetables begin to "sweat" and smell delectable. Remove from oven.
4. Place the roasted ingredients in wok or large skillet. Sauté in a drizzle of olive oil over medium heat. Add a generous sprinkle of salt and basil. Stir continuously for about 3 minutes, or until vegetables are crisp-tender and done to your liking.
5. Serve as a side dish with Italian food, over any sturdy pasta, or along side Tofu Scramble for a colorful brunch or light dinner.

Zucchini with Garlic & Lemon

Serves 4

Preparation and cooking time: 15 minutes

Simple and delicious, this recipe works equally well with tender asparagus, snake beans, broccoli (cut into small florets), and other vegetables. Experiment! Adjust cooking time according to the type of vegetable. Keep in mind that smaller pieces take less time to cook.

2	lb. zucchini (2 medium or 4 small), sliced or cubed	2	Tbsp. fresh herbs (dill, basil, thyme, marjoram, oregano or tarragon), minced
1-2	Tbsp. extra virgin olive oil		salt and pepper
3	garlic cloves , minced	2	tsp. lemon zest, finely grated

1. Heat olive oil in wok or large skillet. Add garlic, then zucchini. Sauté about 4 minutes (time depends on size of the cubes or slices of zucchini).
2. Salt and pepper to taste, then toss with fresh herbs and lemon zest.

Emerald-Sesame Kale

Serves 4

Preparation and cooking time: 10 minutes

High in calcium, Vitamin K, iron, and beta-carotene, kale is a powerhouse vegetable that also tastes great and is easy to prepare. It shrinks dramatically during cooking, so start out with much more than you think you need. A hint of sesame and garlic enlivens this humble vegetable.

4	bunches kale (any variety)	½-1	tsp. dark sesame oil
2-3	garlic cloves, finely minced	1	tsp. Bragg Liquid Aminos
1-2	tsp. toasted sesame seeds		salt (optional)

1. Wash and remove tough stems and ribs of kale. Chop leaves coarsely. Allow at least 6 c. chopped fresh kale per person, as it will shrink to normal serving size as it cooks.
2. Place pile of wet kale in large skillet or wok. Add garlic cloves. Steam-fry over medium heat (do not add liquid), lifting and stirring frequently until kale begins to shrink (chopsticks are good cooking utensils for this). Cover and allow to steam for about 2 minutes, or until kale is wilted and bright green.
(Note: Cooking time depends on variety of kale; delicate Red Russian kale cooks in moments, while the sturdy lacinato and curly varieties take slightly longer.)
3. Drizzle lightly with Bragg Liquid Aminos. Drizzle with a few drops dark sesame oil. Toss gently to coat.
4. Sprinkle with toasted sesame seeds and serve while kale is still bright green.

VARIATION: Swiss Chard may be substituted for all or part of the kale. Reduce cooking time. Chard is more delicate than kale and cooks more quickly.

Carrots with Sea Vegetables

Serves 3-4

Preparation time: 5 minutes   Cooking time: 10 minutes

Rich in iron, minerals, and beta-carotene, this flavorful Japanese-inspired dish is great with brown rice.

2	c. dried arame (sea vegetable)	2	tsp. dark sesame oil
4	carrots, cut into matchsticks	2	tsp. Bragg Liquid Aminos
2-inch piece ginger root, peeled		2	tsp. toasted sesame seeds
	and cut into matchsticks		

1. Cover arame with water and soak for 3 minutes. Drain.
2. Heat sesame oil in wok or large skillet. Add carrots and ginger. Stir-fry 2 minutes.
3. Add drained arame and cook about 5 minutes more, stirring with chopsticks or tossing frequently.
4. Add Bragg Liquid Aminos and cook down until liquid is almost gone.
5. Garnish with toasted sesame seeds.

Carrots & Parsnips

Serves 2-4

Preparation time: 5 minutes   Cooking time: 10 minutes

This colorful, substantial side dish is a delicious source of potassium, beta-carotene, folic acid and Vitamin E.

2	medium carrots, sliced diagonally	1	Tbsp. extra virgin olive oil
1	medium-small parsnip, sliced diagonally	¼	tsp. sea salt
1	bunch parsley or cilantro (about 1 c.), chopped		

1. Place carrots and parsnip in about 1 inch of water in saucepan. Bring to boil, cover and let steam about 10 minutes.
2. Drain cooking water, keeping vegetables in pot. Place pot over low heat. Add olive oil and salt to taste. Stir to coat vegetables.
3. Add chopped parsley or cilantro, stir again, and cook less than 1 minute. Serve hot.

VARIATION: For an Asian twist, omit olive oil and substitute 2 tsp. dark sesame oil. Add a sliver of fresh ginger to cooking pot when steaming veggies, or sauté ginger in sesame oil with cooked veggies.

Savory Roasted Potatoes with Rosemary Serves 6-8

Preparation time: 10 minutes   Roasting time: 25 minutes

Easy, flavorful and aromatic, this uncomplicated dish can be baked along with whatever else is in the oven (see note below about time and temperature). Rosemary adds sophistication and appeal.

3	lb. new red, white, or Yukon Gold potatoes	2	tsp. rosemary
3	garlic cloves		pepper
½	tsp. salt	1	Tbsp. extra virgin olive oil

1. Preheat oven to 450 degrees. Thoroughly scrub potatoes, cut in half, lengthwise, then cut each half, lengthwise again. Cut pieces into chunks about ¾-inch thick. Put into mixing bowl.
2. Smash garlic cloves with flat surface of knife blade. Peel, mince, and sprinkle garlic over potato chunks.
3. Add salt, rosemary, and a few grinds of black pepper. Drizzle extra virgin olive oil over everything. Mix well to coat evenly.
4. Line baking pan with foil or baking parchment. Spread potatoes evenly in single layer and roast 15 minutes. Remove from oven, stir potatoes, and continue roasting for 5 to 10 minutes longer or until golden and tender.

Savory Sweet Potatoes with Rosemary   Serves 6-8

Preparation Time: 10 minutes   Roasting time: 30 minutes

Follow directions for Savory Roasted Potatoes with Rosemary, substituting well-scrubbed sweet potatoes or yams and omitting garlic. The sweet-savory contrast is enhanced by aromatic rosemary. An easy, unusual side dish, this also works well as an appetizer or snack.

VARIATION: Toss with fresh chopped mint, thyme, and/or tarragon instead of rosemary.

(Note: Savory Sweet Potatoes and Savory Roasted Potatoes can be roasted at any temperature between 350 to 450 degrees if using oven for other dishes. Adjust roasting time accordingly, allowing more time for lower temperature. Leftovers may be reheated in covered casserole in oven or microwave.)

HOW TO TOAST SEEDS AND NUTS

METHOD ONE

Spread a single layer of nuts or seeds on parchment-lined baking sheet and bake at 350 degrees until golden or toasty smelling. This will probably take about 10 minutes, depending on type of nuts or seeds. Those with higher fat content may burn more quickly, so be careful! This method works well with pecans and most nuts.

METHOD TWO

In a nonstick frying pan or cast iron skillet, spread a layer of nuts or seeds and "cook" over medium-high heat, stirring frequently until seeds/nuts smell toasty and turn golden, but not dark, brown. This method works best for most seeds, especially sesame seeds. They are done when they start to make popping sounds.

Roasted Root Vegetables with Herbs

Serves a crowd

Preparation time: 5 minutes or less

Roasting time: about 1 hour, depending on type and quantity of vegetable

Roasting brings out the true flavors of most vegetables. The method is simple and the results are delicious.

VEGETABLES: (choose any or all)

carrot	parsnip	squash (butternut, acorn, etc.)
yam	beet	onion (purple, white, or yellow)
potato	sweet potato (any kind)	garlic (whole head, unpeeled)

COATING:

1-2	Tbsp. extra virgin olive oil	¼-½	tsp. salt
2	tsp. rosemary or oregano		

1. Wash, trim, peel, if necessary, and cut into large bite-size chunks your choice of above vegetables.
2. Heat oven to 375 degrees. Place all veggies (except garlic) in large bowl. Drizzle with olive oil. Toss gently to coat. Add rosemary or oregano. Salt liberally. Toss lightly again.
3. Place in single layer on foil-lined baking sheet. Roast until tender and aromatic (do not scorch!). Enjoy as a side dish or with toothpicks as an appetizer.

Mashed Yams Pure & Simple

Allow 1 yam per person

Preparation and cooking time: 30-45 minutes, depending on size of yams

I never understood why a perfectly sweet, delicious yam "needed" to have sugar, pineapples, marshmallows, and other strange things added before it could be eaten. This recipe proves that yams taste great without these embellishments. Great as a side dish for a holiday feast, these yams are the easiest, tastiest yams you will ever prepare.

yams (1 per person)
Butter Buds or Molly McButter
salt

1. Select good yams with no bruises or scars. Scrub well. Boil whole, unpeeled, in large pot until very tender. (Pierce with knife to check.)
2. When cooked, transfer yams to ice bath. Remove peels with fingers—peels should slip right off in your hands. Place peeled yams in large bowl.
3. Sprinkle generously with Butter Buds or Molly McButter. Use electric mixer to mash yams. Salt to taste.
4. Transfer to casserole. Cover and reheat in oven or microwave. DO NOT ADD ANYTHING!

Chopped Broccoli

Serves 4

Preparation time: 5 minutes

Cooking time: 5 minutes

The secret is in the chopping. Small bits of broccoli cook much faster and absorb surrounding flavors more readily. Lemon juice makes this dish sparkle with flavor. One head of broccoli serves one or two people, depending on the size of the broccoli and the size of your appetite.

2-3　broccoli heads
extra virgin olive oil

fresh lemon juice
salt and pepper

1. Thoroughly wash broccoli. Chop broccoli into very small florets. Peel and dice stems.
2. Fill pot with 1 inch water. Place steamer basket in pot. Place broccoli in steamer. Cover and bring water to boil. Steam several minutes, until broccoli is crisp-tender and bright green.
3. Remove steamed broccoli from pot and place in serving bowl. Drizzle lightly with extra virgin olive oil and freshly squeezed lemon juice to taste (see How to Fork a Lemon). Season with salt and freshly ground black pepper to taste. Gently toss.

The Main Event

Many of these entrées are basically one-dish meals.
They provide complete protein by combining
whole grains, legumes, and nuts or seeds. Serve
with a green salad containing nuts or beans, and a
crusty loaf of whole-grain bread. Spread the bread
with any high-protein spread in this book. When
serving a low-protein pasta as an entrée, enjoy a
tofu-based treat or Kashi® Candy for dessert for
added protein.

Herbed Quinoa with Peas & Nuts

Serves 4

Preparation time: 10 minutes

Cooking time: 30-35 minutes

Native to Peru, quinoa ("keen-wah") is an excellent source of plant protein and minerals. Be careful to rinse it thoroughly in a fine sieve under cool running water to remove the bitter coating before cooking. Quinoa has a delicious flavor and intriguing appearance—a tiny spiral encircles each grain when it is cooked. Carrot juice imparts brilliant color and a slightly sweet flavor to this dish.

1	c. quinoa	1	c. carrot juice
1	small onion (about 1 c.), diced	1	c. frozen baby peas (put in sieve and rinse under cool water)
2	small zucchini (about 2-3 c.), diced	½	tsp. salt
½	c. walnuts		pepper
1	Tbsp. plus 1 Tbsp. extra virgin olive oil	2	Tbsp. cilantro or mint
1	tsp. Bragg Liquid Aminos		
2	c. water plus ½ c. water		

1. Thoroughly rinse quinoa in fine sieve under cool running water. Do not skip this essential step!
2. Toast walnuts (see How to Toast Seeds and Nuts). Boil 2 c. water.
3. Saute onion in 1 Tbsp. olive oil in medium saucepan. Cook 2 minutes or until translucent. Do not burn!
4. Stir in quinoa. Add boiling water and Bragg Liquid Aminos. Reduce heat, cover, and cook for 15 minutes.
5. Heat 1 Tbsp. olive oil in skillet. Sauté zucchini over medium heat for 2 minutes. Add carrot juice, ½ c. water, peas, and salt. Cover and simmer 2 minutes.
6. Combine cooked vegetables with cooked quinoa. Gently toss with toasted walnuts. Add freshly ground pepper and more salt, if needed. Garnish with cilantro or mint.

Quinoa, a grain-like crop grown for its edible seeds, is closely related to beets, spinach, chard, and tumbleweeds! A complete protein, this versatile food was cultivated by the Incas and served as the primary protein source in their diet. It is often called "The Gold of the Incas."

Quinoa Stuffed Bell Peppers

Serves 4-6 (one pepper per serving)

Preparation and cooking time: 50 minutes

Baking time: 30 minutes

High in protein, minerals, fiber, and flavor, this colorful dish makes a beautiful centerpiece for a festive table. Use a variety of colors of bell peppers—red, yellow, orange, purple, and even green if the other colors are not available. Quinoa is available in health food stores. Be careful not to overcook or use too much liquid, or quinoa will, quite literally, turn to mush and be more like breakfast porridge.

⅔	c. quinoa	1	small zucchini, diced
2	tsp. plus 2 tsp. extra virgin olive oil	1	(15 oz.) can or 1½ c. cooked garbanzo beans, drained and rinsed
1	tsp. curry powder		
1¼	c. very hot water	¼	c. walnut pieces, toasted (optional)
1	Tbsp. Bragg Liquid Aminos	4-6	large bell peppers (several colors, if possible)
1	medium purple onion, diced		

1. Thoroughly rinse quinoa in fine sieve under cool running water. Do not skip this step!
2. Heat 2 tsp. extra virgin olive oil in large pot over medium heat. Stir in rinsed quinoa and curry powder. Cook 1 minute. Slowly add hot water (almost boiling) and Bragg Liquid Aminos. Reduce heat, cover, and simmer 20 to 25 minutes or until liquid is absorbed. Quinoa should be moist but not mushy.
3. Heat 2 tsp. extra virgin olive oil in skillet over medium heat. Add diced onion and zucchini and cook until onion is translucent, about 3 minutes. Add to quinoa mixture. Preheat oven to 375 degrees.
4. Add beans to quinoa. Add toasted walnut pieces. Stir gently until just combined.
5. Cut tops off bell peppers about 1 inch from top. Reserve tops. Remove seeds and ribs inside peppers. Lightly oil the outside of each pepper, including the tops. Spoon quinoa stuffing into peppers, mounding slightly. Replace tops.
6. Line baking dish with parchment. Arrange bell peppers upright in baking dish. Bake uncovered about 20 minutes, or until peppers are somewhat tender. Be careful not to burn them!
7. Remove from oven. Let stand 10 minutes. Carefully transfer peppers from pan to serving platter using slotted spoon or spatula. Arrange artfully and surround with brightly steamed green vegetable such as broccoli, or create a "nest" of fresh kale for the bell peppers.

CASSEROLE VARIATION: Instead of stuffing the peppers, serve stuffing as a casserole or side dish. Follow recipe for Quinoa Stuffed Bell Peppers, adding 1 diced red bell pepper. Baking is optional.

SALAD VARIATION: Slice ½ red bell pepper into rings. Dice the other half. Stir diced red bell pepper and ½ c. sliced water chestnuts into quinoa mixture. Chill. Serve chilled casserole on a bed of fresh spinach, romaine, or baby greens. Garnish with rings of red bell pepper and a sprinkle of toasted walnuts or pine nuts. Drizzle lightly with extra virgin olive oil or a squeeze of lemon, or Ginger-Lime-Dill Dressing.

ABOUT BELL PEPPERS

All bell peppers start out green. As they mature, their color turns from green to yellow, orange, red, or purple, depending on the variety of pepper. Green peppers are immature, and because they spend less time on the vine their flavor and nutrient content have not fully developed. Mature bell peppers (i.e. any color but green) have considerably more Vitamin C, sweeter flavor, and a higher price.

Stuffed Kabocha Pumpkins

Serves 10-12

Preparation and cooking time: 1 hour   Baking time: 45 minutes

This unusual entrée is a perfect centerpiece for a vegetarian Thanksgiving feast. Stuffed with an assortment of ingredients not normally featured in the same recipe, this delights the senses and satisfies the soul.

1½	c. Lundberg's wild rice blend	½	loaf sourdough bread
½	tsp. salt		Cavender's Greek Seasoning OR salt and
2	kabocha pumpkins		Italian herb blend
1	onion, diced	1	c. cranberries (fresh or frozen, not dried)
4	celery stalks (with leaves), diced	1	c. walnut pieces
1	large portabella mushroom, diced	2	tsp. Bragg Liquid Aminos
2	tsp. extra virgin olive oil	1½	c. warm water

1. Cook Lundberg's wild rice blend in 2½ c. water and ½ tsp. salt.
2. Meanwhile, cut hole in top of kabocha pumpkins and remove seeds, as if preparing a jack-o'-lantern. Keep tops for lids.
3. Sauté onion, celery, and portabella in olive oil until tender. Lightly season with Cavender's Greek Seasoning or salt and Italian herb blend.
4. Tear sourdough bread into chunks and put into large mixing bowl. (Important: Use only very sour sourdough bread with no added fat, sugar, or preservatives—not the kind that comes in cellophane or plastic. Safeway Artisan sourdough works well. Day-old sourdough is preferred.) Sprinkle lightly with Cavender's Greek Seasoning OR salt and Italian herb blend.
5. Combine cooked rice with sourdough. Add sautéed vegetables, portabella, and cooking liquid. Toss gently.
6. Add cranberries and walnut pieces. Toss again.
7. Make "broth" by squirting Bragg Liquid Aminos into warm water. Drizzle slowly over stuffing mixture to moisten. Don't let mixture get too soggy. (May need a little less or a little more, you decide.) Taste stuffing and adjust seasoning, if necessary.
8. Stuff into prepared kabocha pumpkins, filling right to the very top. Place lids on top, place kabochas on baking sheet, and bake in preheated 350 degree oven for about 45 minutes or until kabocha flesh is tender and stuffing is starting to swell. Any remaining stuffing may be baked in casserole for 20 to 30 minutes.
9. Serve as the centerpiece, with lid slightly cocked to show stuffing. If desired, serve with Mushroom-Garlic Gravy and traditional Thanksgiving side dishes.

Mushroom-Garlic Gravy

Preparation and cooking time 15 minutes

Intensely flavored and low-fat, this rich-tasting gravy can be used in place of any meat-based gravy. It looks weird but tastes wonderful!

8-10	oz. fresh mushrooms (any kind), sliced		1	large portabella mushroom, diced
1½	Tbsp. arrowroot starch or cornstarch		5	garlic cloves, peeled and minced
1-2	tsp. Bragg Liquid Aminos		2	tsp. extra virgin olive oil
	salt and pepper			

1. In large skillet, sauté all mushrooms and garlic in olive oil. Don't crowd the mushrooms or they will not brown properly. Stir gently, as needed. Keep lid on when not stirring. Turn heat to low and simmer several minutes.
2. In small glass, mix arrowroot starch or cornstarch with ½ c. cool water until starch is dissolved. Or use small jar with tight-fitting lid and shake the starch and water mixture until starch is dissolved.
3. When mushrooms are tender and juices are flowing, add starch and water mixture and stir well.
4. Add a squirt of Bragg Liquid Aminos and cook until bubbly. If gravy is too thick, add a little water.
5. Use hand-held immersion blender to purée some of the mushrooms in the gravy. Salt and pepper to taste.

Never soak fresh mushrooms or they will become soggy. Before use, simply wipe mushrooms with slightly damp paper towel. Trim stems. For a portabella, break off entire stem and discard it. Portabella stems are very tough, woody, and unappealing in texture and flavor.

Quick Lump-Free Gravy

Yield: 3-4 cups

Preparation time: less than 5 minutes, if rice is already cooked

This delicious, nutritious gravy is high in fiber and B vitamins, tastes rich and creamy, is virtually fat-free, and is always lump-free. The secret is a high-speed blender and cooked short-grain brown rice.

¾	c. cooked short-grain brown rice	2	c. very warm water or broth
1	tsp. Bragg Liquid Aminos		salt and pepper

1. In blender, combine brown rice, a generous squirt of Bragg Liquid Aminos, and warm water or broth. Blend on high until smooth. If necessary, add more rice, a little at a time, and continue blending until desired thickness is achieved and gravy is absolutely silken and creamy. Stop blender and test gravy every 20 seconds.
2. Pour blended gravy into pan and heat up, stirring frequently. For thinner gravy, add a little more liquid and blend until smooth. Salt and pepper to taste and serve over grains, vegetables, or (for carnivores) meat or poultry.

Mixed Grain Pilaf
with Walnuts & Garbanzos

Serves 4

Preparation and cooking time: 1 hour

Great as a side dish or fortified with garbanzo beans as a main dish, this versatile pilaf provides protein, fiber, B vitamins, and satisfying flavor. Experiment with various grains and nuts.

1	onion, diced	3½	c. water or vegetable broth
2	celery stalks (with leaves), diced	1	(15 oz.) can or 1½ c. cooked garbanzo beans, drained and rinsed
1	Tbsp. extra virgin olive oil		
1½	c. long-grain brown rice	¼ -½	c. toasted walnuts
¼	c. barley	1	lemon (for zest and juice)
¼	c. wild rice	2	Tbsp. fresh mint, chopped or torn

1. In large skillet with tight-fitting lid, heat olive oil. Sauté onion and celery about 2 minutes, until translucent.
2. Measure rices and barley into skillet. Cover with water or vegetable broth. Salt liberally. Cover, bring to boil then reduce heat to simmer. Do not disturb for 45 minutes.
3. Zest lemon (use a Microplane if available). Stir in beans, nuts, and 1 tsp. lemon zest before serving. Fork the lemon and squeeze juice over everything. Add mint, toss gently, and serve.

VARIATION: For a quick and easy version, use packaged rice blend (Lundberg's wild rice blend is good) instead of mixed grains. Cook according to package directions. Or use brown rice or any combination of whole grains, totaling 2 c. uncooked. Try different fresh herbs and your choice of toasted nuts.

Confetti Stir-Fry

Serves 4-6

Preparation and cooking time: 30 minutes, use cooked rice

This tasty, easy, colorful dish is an excellent way to use fresh vegetables and cooked rice from last night's meal. Alternatively, serve over rice noodles. Variations are limitless. The key to this dish is slicing the vegetables into uniformly small pieces for quick cooking and easier eating. Wash and prepare all vegetables BEFORE starting to cook!

½	block (8-10 oz.) firm tofu (in water)	¾	c. mushrooms (may use canned straw mushrooms or golden mushrooms)
¼	purple onion, sliced into strips		
3	garlic cloves, peeled and minced	2	c. mung bean sprouts
1-inch piece ginger root, peeled and finely minced		1	(5 oz.) can sliced water chestnuts
		3	c. fresh greens (spinach, tat soi, won bok, chard), chopped
2	tsp. extra virgin olive oil		
1	small head broccoli, divided into small florets	¾	c. purple cabbage, finely shredded
1	small zucchini, cut into matchsticks	3-4	c. cooked long-grain brown rice or rice noodles
½	carrot (about ¼ c.), cut into matchsticks		Bragg Liquid Aminos
		¼	tsp. dark sesame oil
			sriracha hot chili sauce

1. Drain tofu. Fold cotton tea-towel in half, lengthwise. Place block of drained tofu at end of towel nearest you. Roll up tofu in towel and let rest until towel is saturated. Unwrap and slice tofu into ¾-inch cubes.
2. In large skillet or wok, sauté garlic, ginger and onion in olive oil for 2 minutes. Add tofu cubes. Sauté 2 minutes, then add vegetables and stir lightly for 1 minute.
3. Squirt with Bragg Liquid Aminos, toss gently, then cover and steam for 1 minute. DO NOT OVERCOOK or cabbage will discolor and look disgusting. Add several drops sesame oil.
4. If using rice noodles, add prepared noodles to vegetables and toss well with a dab of sriracha.

Vegetarian Paella

Serves 4-6

Preparation and cooking time: 1 hour

This easy one-dish meal looks spectacular if served immediately. Do not make this ahead of time or peas will turn ugly and unappetizing.

2   c. short-grain brown rice
1   (14.5 oz.) can diced tomatoes (with liquid)
Bragg Liquid Aminos
2   tsp. extra virgin olive oil
3   garlic cloves, peeled and minced
½   purple onion, cut into strips
1   red bell pepper, cut into 2-3-inch strips

1   small can sliced mushrooms, drained (optional)
1   small jar artichoke hearts, drained
pinch turmeric (less than ⅛ tsp.)
salt and pepper
1   c. frozen petite peas
fresh parsley

1. In a large pot or rice cooker, combine rice, 1½ c. water, and diced tomatoes with their juices. Add a generous squirt of Bragg Liquid Aminos and close lid. Bring to boil, then simmer on lowest heat for 40 minutes or until done.
2. Lightly coat inside bottom of wok or large skillet with extra virgin olive oil. Add garlic, onion, bell pepper, mushrooms, and artichokes. Sauté over medium heat.
3. When rice is done, add to wok. Sprinkle in turmeric. Stir well. (Turmeric turns everything yellow as it heats up, so don't use too much!) Salt and pepper to taste.
4. Put frozen peas in strainer and run cool tap water over them to remove any ice crystals. Just before serving, mix peas to paella mixture. Do not cover after peas have been added. Garnish with a scattering of fresh parsley. Serve immediately.

In the 16th century, artichokes were believed to be aphrodisiacs, and women were forbidden to eat them.

Rice Ring Mold

Serves 6

Preparation and cooking time: 1 hour

A novel way of presenting paella, this easy ring mold looks good enough to be a centerpiece for a fancy meal.

1. Prepare Vegetarian Paella, omitting peas. Dissolve 2 Tbsp. nutritional yeast flakes in ¾ c. water. Stir into paella. Keep stirring until paella turns slightly sticky.
2. Lightly spray or coat inside of Bundt pan or ring mold with olive oil. Press paella mixture firmly into mold. Invert mold onto serving platter.
3. Fill center of mold with brightly steamed broccoli florets. Surround platter with more steamed broccoli and fresh cherry tomatoes.

German-Style Scalloped Potatoes

Serves 4

Preparation time: 30 minutes, if using processor or slicer   Baking time: 45 minutes

Rich, creamy, and satisfying, this dish is truly comfort food. Sauerkraut is the key ingredient, so don't skimp. The recipe contains virtually no fat and tastes too good to be legal! Use a mandolin or food processor to cut the potatoes and onion paper-thin and make preparation much quicker and easier.

2   large potatoes (about 4-5 c. total)
1   jar sauerkraut (3-4 c. total)
pepper
veggie ham or veggie Canadian bacon
1   large onion

1   Tbsp. whole wheat pastry flour or
      unbleached white flour
¾   c. nutritional yeast
2   Tbsp. white (mellow) miso

1. Peel and thinly slice potatoes, about 4 or 5 c. Make slices almost paper-thin. Slice onion into rings using the same mandolin or slicer.
2. Spray or lightly coat large (about 3 to 4 inches deep) oblong baking dish or casserole with olive oil. Place layer of sauerkraut (do not drain) on bottom of pan. Sprinkle with pepper.
3. Cover sauerkraut with even layer of sliced potatoes (about 2 c.). Cover potatoes with layer of veggie ham or veggie Canadian bacon and onion rings.
4. Cover with another layer of sauerkraut, then a thin layer of potatoes. Sprinkle with flour.
5. Add another thin layer of onion rings, veggie "meats," or both. Top with remaining potato slices.
6. In blender, combine and blend nutritional yeast and miso with 2 c. water. Preheat oven to 375 degrees.
7. Pour blended mixture over potato mixture. Sprinkle with paprika or freshly-ground black pepper.
8. Cover and bake for about 45 minutes or until potatoes are tender but not mushy. (The shallower the pan, the shorter the baking time.

To summarize: Thinly layer in order, starting from bottom of pan: sauerkraut, potato slices, veggie "meat," onion rings, sauerkraut, potato slices, flour, veggie "meat," onion rings, potato slices, miso-nutritional yeast sauce, paprika, or pepper.

VARIATIONS: Try layering red bell pepper rings and/or sautéed mushrooms instead of veggie "meats" and onion rings. A generous sprinkling of dill weed throughout the layers adds a delightful flavor. Experiment with other types of vegetarian "meats," if you wish.

Tofu-Spinach Balls

Serves 3-4

Preparation time: 30 minutes

Baking time: 30 minutes

Easier than it looks, the trick is to let the oven do the work. Drain and wrap the tofu the night before if you prefer. The mixture may be made a day or two ahead and refrigerated. The sauce is high in fat (the good kind), and the entire dish is a great source of calcium and protein. For variety, experiment with different sauces. Serve over brown rice or other cooked whole grains.

1 block (16-20 oz.) extra-firm tofu	1 tsp. curry powder
5 oz. frozen chopped spinach (½ box or ¼ bag)	1 Tbsp. Bragg Liquid Aminos
3 Tbsp. nutritional yeast flakes	1 Tbsp. arrowroot starch or garbanzo flour

1. Cut tofu in half, lengthwise. Wrap each half snugly in cotton tea-towel until towel is thoroughly saturated. Repeat with fresh dry towel.
2. Put spinach in fine-mesh strainer. Rinse gently under running water to loosen and thaw. Drain well and squeeze dry. (Should be about ½ c. packed spinach). Put in medium bowl.
3. Preheat oven to 350 degrees. Unwrap tofu and crumble into bowl with spinach. Add nutritional yeast flakes, Bragg Liquid Aminos, curry powder, and arrowroot starch or garbanzo flour.
4. Mash well with fork or mix everything in food processor. Press firmly into ¼ c. mold (mixture will be moist and airy and won't hold its shape until baked). Unmold onto parchment-lined baking sheet and bake in oven for 25 minutes. Do not attempt this without parchment. There is no satisfactory substitute!!!
5. Remove tofu balls from oven. Carefully place them in shallow casserole. Pour sauce over everything, completely covering tofu balls. (It will look like there is too much sauce, but this is the right amount.) Cover casserole and return to oven for 5 minutes. Serve with Tahini-Garlic Sauce.

Instant Vegetarian Chili

Serves 6-8

Preparation time: 5 minutes

Cooking time: 15 minutes

This chili tastes like the cook slaved for hours, but it is almost instant and relies on canned ingredients. Buy the best-quality canned beans (organic, if possible) and avoid beans with added sugar or sweetener. The dry vegetarian chili mix with TVP can be bought in bulk at most health food stores. If using an automatic rice cooker, switch to "warm" setting as soon as chili comes to a boil. Chili will stay warm and keep all day.

1	(15 oz.) can kidney beans, drained and rinsed
1	(15 oz.) can pinto beans or black beans, drained and rinsed
1	(15 oz.) can fat-free refried beans (any kind)
1	small jar chunky salsa, southwestern style (with corn, peppers, onions, etc.)
1	c. vegetarian chili mix with TVP (textured vegetable protein)
1	(15 oz.) can tomatoes, ready-cut
¼	tsp. crushed red chili pepper flakes (or to taste)

OPTIONAL VEGGIES:

1	small zucchini, diced	1	celery stalk (with leaves), sliced
1	onion, diced	1	(11 oz.) can corn
1	bell pepper (any color), diced	1	small can sliced mushrooms

1. Combine all beans, salsa, chili mix, tomatoes, and chili pepper in large pot over medium heat and stir well.
2. Cover. When chili starts to boil, turn heat to low and add optional veggies (any or all). Simmer 10 minutes or until ready to serve.
3. Add water or tomato juice if chili is too thick. Adjust seasonings to taste. Serve with Corn Bread (see Bread and Breakfast) or brown rice.

VARIATIONS: To make soup, add another can of diced tomatoes and all of the "optional" veggies. Thin soup to desired consistency with water or tomato juice.

PASTA BASICS

No matter how good the sauce is, if the pasta is not cooked to perfection, the entire dish is ruined. Here are thirteen secrets of perfect pasta.

1. Cook the correct amount. 1 pound of dry pasta usually serves 4. If tossed with generous amounts of vegetables and other ingredients, it will serve at least 6. Figure that 4 entrée-size servings equal 8 side-dish servings.

2. Use enough water. Fill a large (6 to 8 quart) pot at least ⅔ full of cold water. The pasta needs enough room to cook or it will become gluey and stick together.

3. Bring the water to a full rolling boil. Use high heat and cover the pot.

4. Salt the water after it starts to boil. Up to 2 tsp. salt per pound of pasta really improves flavor. Most of the salt is not absorbed, so by seasoning the water you will actually reduce sodium consumption because you will not have to over-salt at the table.

5. Add the pasta and stir. Do not break up long strands. For long pasta, grab with both hands. Stand pasta upright in the pot. Twist (wringing action) with both hands, then release. Pasta will fan out instead of clumping together. As strands start to soften, gently push them down into the water.

6. Adjust the heat so the water keeps boiling but does not boil over. Cook uncovered, stirring occasionally.

7. Omit the oil. Oil makes it harder for sauces to cling.

8. Cook al denté—until pasta is slightly resistant to the bite but not soft. Test a single piece by biting into it. When done, drain immediately. For a more intense flavor and integrated dish, undercook the pasta slightly and add it to the simmering sauce to finish cooking (for about 2 minutes).

9. Save some cooking water. Before draining, reserve up to 1 cup cooking water to add to the sauce if sauce needs thinning or extending.

10. Drain quickly because pasta continues to cook in hot water. Place a large colander in the sink. Pour cooked pasta into colander and shake gently to remove excess water.

11. Do NOT rinse! Rinsing prevents sauces from adhering to pasta. To cool pasta quickly for salads drain it into a colander, then plunge colander into ice water. Drain well.

12. Warm pasta bowls in the oven at 200 degrees if serving hot pasta.

13. Toss pasta with sauce and serve immediately. Have the sauce and other ingredients ready when the pasta is ready and hot. If you wait too long, the pasta will soak up the sauce and become soggy.

Quick & Easy Marinara (Basic Recipe)   Serves 4

Preparation and cooking time: less than 30 minutes

This hearty sauce is the basis for a variety of pasta dishes and can also be used as pizza sauce. Always use canned tomatoes. The tomatoes are picked and canned at their peak of ripeness so their flavor and nutritional value are superior to store-bought "fresh" tomatoes. Unless you have vine-ripened tomatoes growing in your own back yard, stick with canned tomatoes for all your tomato-based pasta sauces. Here is the basic recipe, with variations following. For added protein, serve with a fresh garden salad topped with garbanzo beans or walnuts instead of croutons.

1 medium onion, diced	½ tsp. sea salt (or more to taste)
4 garlic cloves, peeled and minced	black pepper (few grinds)
2 tsp. plus 1 tsp. extra virgin olive oil	2 Tbsp. fresh herbs (basil, oregano, thyme,
1 (14.5 oz.) can tomatoes, diced or crushed	marjoram, etc.)
1 tsp. oregano or Italian seasoning blend	½ tsp. sugar or agave nectar (optional)
1 Tbsp. fresh basil, chopped OR	
1 tsp. dried basil	

1. In medium pot over medium heat, heat 2 tsp. olive oil. Sauté onion and garlic until translucent, about 3 minutes.
2. Stir in tomatoes (with liquid), oregano (or Italian seasoning), basil, and salt.
3. Bring to boil. Reduce heat to medium-low and cook uncovered about 15 minutes. Taste for seasoning. Add more salt, if necessary. If sauce tastes too acidic, add sugar or agave nectar. Add a few grinds of black pepper.
4. Just before serving, add a light drizzle of extra virgin olive oil (about 1 tsp. or less) and stir gently. Stir in your choice of fresh herbs.
5. Serve in pasta bowls over your choice of cooked, well-drained pasta (cooked al denté). Garnish with fresh parsley or basil.

MUSHROOM MARINARA VARIATION: Follow recipe for Quick & Easy Marinara, sautéing 2 c. sliced or quartered fresh mushrooms with onion and garlic.

Pesto Pasta

Serves 4-6

Preparation and cooking time: 15 minutes

Make the pesto ahead of time and have it on hand for an almost-instant entrée or side dish.

1	lb. linguini	Pine nuts for garnish
2	tsp. salt	Fresh basil or cilantro for garnish
⅓	c. Herb Pesto or Cilantro-Sesame Pesto Dressing	

1. Fill large pot with water and bring to rolling boil. Add salt and linguini. Cook according to package directions. Don't let it boil over and do not overcook!
2. Meanwhile, prepare Herb Pesto or Cilantro-Sesame Pesto Dressing.
3. Drain cooked linguini in colander. Pour hot, drained linguini into large serving bowl and toss with enough pesto to evenly coat.
4. Serve immediately. Garnish with toasted pine nuts or a sprig of fresh basil or cilantro.

Tomato-Tofu Angel Hair

Serves 2-4

Preparation time: 15 minutes or less

Tasty and easy, this dish is even quicker if the Tomato-Tofu Relish is made ahead.

8	oz. angel hair pasta	1½ c. Tomato-Tofu Relish
1	tsp. salt	fresh basil for garnish

1. Fill medium pot ⅔ full of water and bring to rolling boil.
2. Add salt and angel hair pasta to boiling water. (Grab handful of angel hair pasta with both hands, stand it upright in the middle of the pot of boiling water, twist it with a wringing action, and release pasta into the boiling water. Pasta should "fan" out like a daisy.) Pasta will gradually all sink into the boiling water.
3. Cook pasta briefly according to package directions. When done al denté, drain well in colander over the sink.
4. Toss with Tomato-Tofu Relish. Garnish with fresh basil. Serve immediately.

Tomatoes are one of the only foods whose nutritional value is actually increased by cooking or processing. More lycopene is absorbed by the body from cooked tomatoes than from fresh tomatoes. In fact, cooked tomatoes deliver three times more lycopene to the body than the equivalent amount of fresh tomatoes!

"Meat" Sauce

Serves 4

This sauce fools even the most meat-loving palate. The soy adds protein, texture, and flavor.

⅓ c. ground-beef-style soy protein (dry)
⅓ c. boiling water

Bragg Liquid Aminos
Quick & Easy Marinara (full recipe)

1. In small bowl, add boiling water to ground-beef-style soy protein (TVP). Add a generous squirt of Bragg Liquid Aminos. Let rest 5 minutes or until all liquid is absorbed.
2. Add this reconstituted soy protein to Quick & Easy Marinara. Simmer at least 15 minutes.
3. Serve in pasta bowls over your choice of well-drained, al denté pasta. Garnish with fresh parsley or basil.

Zucchini-Portabella Pasta with Marinara Sauce

Serves 4

Preparation and cooking time: 15 minutes, if Marinara Sauce is already made or if bottled sauce is used

Fast and delicious! Serve with crusty Italian bread and a salad of romaine and garbanzo beans (for protein), tossed with vinaigrette.

1 small zucchini, cut into matchsticks

mushroom, stemmed
     and cut into ½-inch cubes
3 c. Quick & Easy Marinara Sauce
2 garlic cloves, minced

½ lb. rigatoni or penne
1 large portabella
2 tsp. plus ½ tsp. salt
2 tsp. plus 1 tsp. extra
     virgin olive oil
1 Tbsp. balsamic vinegar

Portabella mushrooms are overgrown (mature) crimini mushrooms.

1. Fill large pot ⅔ full of water. Bring water to boil.
2. When water is at rolling boil, add 2 tsp. salt and pasta. Cook according to package directions, being careful not to let it boil over.
3. Meanwhile, in large skillet or wok (wok is best if you have one) over medium heat, sauté garlic, portabella, and zucchini in olive oil. Salt lightly.
4. When juices from portabella begin to flow and zucchini is almost tender, add Quick & Easy Marinara Sauce and balsamic vinegar. Stir to combine.
5. Remove pasta from stove just before it is done. Drain thoroughly in colander. Add drained pasta to sauce and stir well. If necessary, add a little more sauce.
6. Just before serving, drizzle a little extra virgin olive oil over everything. Serve hot.

VARIATION: Instead of using Quick & Easy Marinara Sauce, substitute a good-quality, low-fat, sugar-free bottled pasta sauce such as Classico brand tomato and basil sauce.

HOW TO PIT OLIVES AND PEEL GARLIC

Place olives or individual garlic cloves on cutting board. Place the flat blade of a large (wide-blade) sharp knife on an olive or garlic clove and smash down. Olive pit should come out easily. Garlic clove should slide out of the papery peel. After removing pits, chop olives or garlic with same knife, using both hands. Hold the knife sideways (not pointing forward), with handle in your right hand (or left hand if you are left-handed). With sharp side facing down, hold the top of other end of knife blade with the other palm of other hand, pressing down on cutting board. Keeping tip end of blade on the cutting board, this becomes a pivot and the chopping is done by moving the handle end of the blade over the garlic (or whatever needs to be chopped) in a chopping motion while holding down the tip end. Chop, chop!

Roma Tomato-Arugula-Olive Vermicelli — Serves 2-3

Preparation and cooking time: 30 minutes or less

Quick, easy, and beautiful, this garden-fresh dish should be eaten immediately.

½	c. Kalamata olives, pitted and chopped	1-2	Tbsp. extra virgin olive oil
2-3	Roma tomatoes, diced	8	oz. angel hair or vermicelli
3-4	c. arugula, coarsely chopped		salt
2-3	Tbsp. balsamic vinegar		pepper

(Note: Roma tomatoes are preferred, but other ripe tomatoes may be substituted, if necessary. If using grape or cherry tomatoes, slice them in half.)

1. Combine olives, tomatoes, and arugula in large mixing bowl. Add balsamic vinegar and olive oil. Sprinkle liberally with sea salt. Toss and let sit for 15 minutes until arugula is wilted.
2. Fill medium pot with water, leaving 2 inches head room. Bring water to rolling boil. Add pasta and 2 tsp. salt to boiling water. (Grab handful of noodles with both hands, stand it upright in the middle of pot of boiling water, twist it with a wringing action, and release pasta into boiling water. Pasta should "fan" out like a daisy.) Pasta will gradually all sink into the boiling water. Cook according to package directions until tender, but firm (al denté). This type of pasta cooks very quickly! Drain immediately.
3. Pour hot, drained pasta into bowl with wilted veggies. Toss and serve immediately. Top with coarse freshly ground black pepper.

VARIATIONS: Substitute tender baby spinach or tat soi if arugula is not available. Fresh basil adds a delightful flavor. Linguini or spaghetti can be used if angel hair or vermicelli is not available.

ABOUT PASTA

Pasta provides the perfect solution to a quick, versatile, low-fat, delicious meal. Not just an Italian food, pasta of every sort is part of the cuisines of many cultures around the world. Keep your pantry well-stocked with a variety of pastas in all shapes, sizes, colors, and flavors. For those allergic to wheat, several companies make pastas with corn, rice, spelt, kamut, and other grains. They look the same but the texture and flavor are slightly different when the pasta is cooked. Try various whole grain pastas and organic pastas. Southeast Asian cuisine relies heavily on rice noodles. Experiment with different kinds of pasta in the following recipes. For more intense flavor and a more integrated dish, remove pasta from boiling water just before it is "done," drain thoroughly, and toss it with the simmering sauce for the final few minutes of cooking.

Pantry Pasta

Serves 4-6

Preparation and cooking time: 10-15 minutes

If fresh vegetables are limited and you are in a hurry, this is the perfect solution. Always keep an emergency supply of "special" canned and bottled items in your pantry. They will come in handy when you have unexpected guests, and they keep almost forever.

PASTA:

1	lb. penne, rigatoni, or linguini	1	tsp. salt

VEGETABLE OPTIONS: (choose any or all)

2	garlic cloves, peeled and minced	¼	c. sun-dried tomatoes, chopped
¼	c. olives, pitted and chopped, or sliced	1	small jar artichoke hearts, drained and quartered
1-2	Tbsp. capers	⅓	c. roasted red bell peppers (in jar), chopped

ENHANCEMENTS:

½	tsp. Italian herb blend or other dried herbs	2-3	Tbsp. toasted pine nuts OR walnut pieces
1	Tbsp. extra virgin olive oil		fresh oregano, basil or other Italian herbs (optional)
2	Tbsp. balsamic vinegar or lemon juice		salt and pepper

1. Bring water to rolling boil in large pot. Add your favorite sturdy pasta and salt. Cook according to package directions. Do not overcook.
2. In large frying pan or wok, heat olive oil. Sauté garlic, olives, artichokes, bell pepper, sun-dried tomatoes, and capers for 1 minute or until just heated through.

3. Drain cooked pasta in colander over sink. Do not rinse. Add drained pasta to sautéed veggies.

4. Sprinkle pasta and veggies with herbs. Squeeze juice from ½ lemon OR drizzle balsamic vinegar. Salt and pepper to taste. Toss gently.

5. If desired, top with a few toasted walnuts or pine nuts and/or a few shavings of parmesan (never use pre-grated stuff in can) or other hard cheese. Take a bow!

Balsamic Angel Hair Primavera   Serves 2-3

Preparation and cooking time: 30 minutes

Festive enough for company but simple enough for everyday, this dish takes advantage of the freshest vegetables available. Vegetables may be washed and prepared the day before and stored refrigerated in Ziploc bags or air tight containers until ready to cook.

8 oz. angel hair pasta	2 tsp. salt
VEGETABLE OPTIONS: (choose any or all)	
1 c. snow peas in pod, trim ends	2 c. Swiss chard, chopped
4 stalks thin asparagus, cut diagonally into 1-inch pieces	¼ purple onion, cut into strips
	3 garlic cloves, mashed and peeled
1 c. green or yellow zucchini, cut into thin "half-moons"	2 Tbsp. fresh basil, chopped or chiffonaded
	½ red bell pepper, cut into strips
ENHANCEMENTS:	
1 Tbsp. plus 1 Tbsp. extra virgin olive oil	Cavender's Greek Seasoning (optional)
1 Tbsp. balsamic vinegar	salt and pepper

1. Thoroughly wash and prepare your choice of vegetables listed above.

2. In large nonstick frying pan or wok, sauté garlic and onion in olive oil. Add vegetables. Stir-fry briefly, about 1 minute. Cover with lid and let steam for 2 minutes, until colors are bright and veggies are crisp-tender.

3. Bring large pot of water (at least 2 quarts) to rolling boil. Add 2 tsp. salt. Grab handful of angel hair pasta with both hands, stand it upright in the middle of the pot of boiling water, twist it with a wringing action, and release pasta into boiling water. Pasta should "fan" out like a daisy. Pasta will gradually all sink into the boiling water. Cook for 2 to 3 minutes. Do not overcook! When almost tender, drain in colander and rinse with cool water.

4. Pour drained, rinsed pasta into pan with vegetables. Season liberally with Cavender's Greek Seasoning or salt and freshly ground pepper. Drizzle lightly with olive oil and balsamic vinegar. Toss gently but thoroughly until pasta is heated and everything is lightly coated.

Pasta Confetti

Preparation and cooking time: 20-30 minutes

A great way to use up lonely vegetables, this nutritious, low-fat salad is a delightful medley of color, flavor, and texture. With beans added, it's not only an entrée, but a meal in itself!

VEGETABLES: (choose any or all)

1	head broccoli florets
4	asparagus spears, cut into 1-inch pieces
½	carrot, grated or diced
1	small green or yellow zucchini, diced
1	bell pepper (any color), seeded and diced
1	tomato (very ripe), diced
1	cucumber, diced
½	avocado, diced
2	tsp. salt

⅓	c. olives (any kind) and/or sun-dried tomatoes
1	can (15 oz.) garbanzo beans, drained and well-rinsed
½	c. walnut pieces
1-2	Tbsp. rice vinegar
	salt and pepper
	fresh herbs such as basil, oregano, tarragon or other (optional)
	feta, crumbled (optional)

PASTA:

8-10 oz. pasta (radiatore, shells, or any pasta with texture to "capture" other ingredients)

1. Bring large pot of water to boil. Meanwhile, wash, trim and prepare your choice of vegetables listed above.
2. Add salt to boiling water. Add broccoli and/or asparagus and blanch for a few seconds. Remove from boiling water and immerse into bowl of ice water to stop cooking process and retain bright green color.
3. With water still boiling, add pasta. Cook al denté, according to package directions.
4. Drain and rinse cooked pasta in cold water (to chill). Pour into large serving bowl. Add prepared vegetables.
5. Chop olives and/or sun-dried tomatoes and add to bowl. Add beans and walnut pieces. Toss gently.
6. Sprinkle with rice vinegar. Salt and pepper to taste. If desired, dress with Italian vinaigrette. Toss again.
7. If serving in individual bowls, line bowl with frilly lettuce leaves and top with a little crumbled feta. Sprinkle salad with fresh herbs.

VARIATIONS: Experiment with different types of pastas, herbs, and vegetables. This salad is only limited by your imagination!

Bow Ties with Smoked Tofu & Peas   Serves 4

Preparation and cooking time: 15-20 minutes

White Wave brand hickory smoked barbeque flavor baked tofu makes this dish very quick to prepare. This simple, tasty dish may be served hot as an entrée or chilled as a salad.

12	oz. bow tie pasta (farfalle)	8	oz. baked tofu (hickory smoked barbeque flavor), cubed
1	lemon (to make 2 tsp. lemon zest and 2-3 Tbsp. juice)	5	oz. (½ pkg.) frozen petite peas
2	tsp. extra virgin olive oil	1	tsp. dried dill weed (or up to 1 Tbsp. fresh dill)

1. Fill large pot ⅔ full of water and bring to rolling boil over high heat.
2. Add pasta (farfalle) to boiling water. Stir. Bring back to boil and reduce heat to medium. Do not cover and do not allow it to boil over.
3. Meanwhile, finely grate lemon zest and squeeze juice from ½ lemon.
4. In large nonstick wok or skillet, heat olive oil. Add lemon zest and baked tofu. Toss gently.
5. When pasta is cooked al denté, remove ½ c. pasta cooking water. Add to wok mixture.
6. Pour frozen peas into colander. Rinse under cool running water. Pour cooked pasta into colander over frozen peas. Shake gently to drain.
7. Add pasta and peas to wok. Add dill and lemon juice. Toss or stir gently to combine all ingredients. Serve immediately, while peas are still bright green.

Thai-Style Pasta with Baked Tofu & Peas   Serves 4

Preparation and cooking time: 15-20 minutes

Follow directions for above recipe (Bow Ties with Smoked Tofu & Peas), substituting lime zest and fresh lime juice for lemon. Use White Wave Thai-style baked tofu instead of hickory-smoked barbeque baked tofu. Use rice noodles (rice stick) instead of other pasta.

Rice Stick (Oriental Rice Noodles)

Preparation and cooking time: 5-7 minutes

Ever wonder how to cook rice noodles (rice stick)? They come packaged without directions or the directions are not in English. I learned how to prepare them from my Vietnamese friend, Coi. They are great for a simple soup and ideal for people who cannot tolerate gluten or wheat.

rice noodles

water

1. Fill large pot ⅔ full with water and bring to rolling boil over high heat.
2. Meanwhile, fill large bowl with warm (not hot) water.
3. Soak desired amount of rice noodles (choose narrow, medium or wide "sticks") in bowl or warm water for about 4 minutes. Pour into colander and drain.
4. Dump soaked rice noodles into pot of boiling water. Stir. Remove immediately (within 10 seconds). Pour into colander and drain. Noodles are now ready to use in a variety of recipes such as stir-fry or soup.

Soba-Veggie Stir-Fry

Serves 6

Preparation and cooking time: 30 minutes

Soba noodles are made from buckwheat and offer a nutritious, delicious alternative to other noodles or grains. The sauce adds "zing." Make a trip to an Asian market if you can't find soba or vegetarian stir-fry sauce at your local grocery store. It's worth the effort.

8	oz. soba noodles		1	tsp. ginger root, peeled and finely minced
2	tsp. salt		½	c. snow peas, tips trimmed
2	tsp. extra virgin olive oil or sesame oil		1	small zucchini, cut into half-moons
¼	purple onion, sliced into strips		½	carrot, cut into matchsticks (about ¼ c.)
3	garlic cloves, peeled and minced		2	Tbsp. sesame seeds (garnish)
½	red bell pepper, sliced into 2-inch strips			

SAUCE:

¼	c. spicy V8 juice or tomato sauce		⅛	tsp. dark sesame oil
1	Tbsp. Bragg Liquid Aminos		¼	tsp. dried crushed red pepper flakes
1	Tbsp. vegetarian stir-fry sauce (similar to oyster sauce but without oyster)			

1. Bring at least 2 quarts water to rolling boil. Add soba (buckwheat) noodles and salt. Cook about 6 minutes, stirring occasionally. Do not overcook.
2. In large skillet or wok, sauté garlic, ginger and onion in oil for 2 minutes. Add prepared vegetables and stir-fry lightly until crisp tender and bright, about 2 minutes.
3. In small jar with tight screw-top lid, combine all sauce ingredients and shake well.
4. Drain and rinse cooked soba noodles in colander. Add to vegetable mixture.
5. Pour sauce over everything and toss lightly, using pasta server or chopsticks. Stir-fry only until most of sauce is absorbed and everything is hot. Serve in wok, large bowl, or individual pasta bowls.
6. Toast sesame seeds in dry pan on top of stove until they start to "pop" (less than 1 minute). Sprinkle noodles with toasted sesame seeds and serve with Sesame-Tofu Nuggets (optional). Eat with chopsticks.

> Buckwheat is not a type of wheat, but related to the rhubarb family. A compete protein and rich in iron and B vitamins, the whole grain is also known as kasha. Buckwheat noodles are called soba.

Orzo with Broccoli

Serves 6-8

Preparation and cooking time: 20 minutes

Orzo is a small, rice-shaped pasta that cooks quickly. Fast, easy, and versatile, this dish works well as a side dish, salad, or entrée for a light lunch.

1	broccoli head		1	(15 oz.) can or 1½ c. cooked garbanzo beans (optional)
2	c. orzo (white or multicolored)			salt and pepper
12	Kalamata olives, pitted and chopped			
2	Tbsp. sun-dried tomatoes (in jar), chopped		2-3	Tbsp. rice vinegar
				extra virgin olive oil
½	c. walnut pieces			fresh herbs for garnish (optional)

1. Cut broccoli into small florets. Peel and dice stems.
2. Bring at least 2 quarts water to rolling boil. Add 1 tsp. salt and broccoli. Blanch broccoli for almost 1 minute, until bright green and crisp-tender.
3. With slotted spoon or strainer, remove broccoli from boiling water and plunge into bowl of ice water. (This stops the cooking process and retains the bright green color.)
4. Add orzo, bring water back to boiling and cook about 5 minutes. Do not to overcook or it will turn to mush.
5. Drain chilled broccoli in colander, then transfer to large serving bowl.
6. Drain cooked orzo in same colander. Rinse under cool, running water. Drain well and add to serving bowl. Drain and rinse garbanzo beans.
7. Add olives, sun-dried tomatoes, garbanzo beans, and walnut pieces to bowl. Toss gently.
8. Sprinkle with rice vinegar (do not substitute!!). Salt and pepper to taste.
9. Immediately before serving, drizzle lightly with extra virgin olive oil. As salad, serve on a bed of romaine or other lettuces (not iceberg). If desired, crumble a little feta on top, or garnish with fresh basil.

Fettuccine Alfredo (very lowfat)

Serves 4

Preparation and cooking time: 30 minutes, if garlic is already roasted, 40 minutes if not

The ultimate in comfort food, this creamy pasta contains no cream, eggs, milk, butter, or oil. High in protein, fiber, and vitamins (including Vitamin B$_{12}$), this delicious dish is actually very good for you! Cannellini, Great Northern, navy, or other white beans (not lima beans) may be used.

1-2	large garlic heads (the whole head)	¼	c. nutritional yeast
2	broccoli heads	15	oz. plain soymilk (use empty bean can to measure)
10-12	oz. fettuccini		
3	sun-dried tomatoes (dry, not bottled)	1½	tsp. plus ¾ tsp. salt
⅓	c. hot water (from cooking pasta)	½	tsp. ground turmeric
2	(15 oz.) cans or 3 c. cooked cannellini or navy beans, with liquid		

1. Separate garlic cloves but do not peel them. Toast garlic in nonstick skillet over medium-low heat for exactly 8 minutes, stirring frequently. Garlic should be somewhat tender and aromatic. Meanwhile...

2. Cut broccoli into bite-size florets. Peel and dice stems. Then peel the toasted garlic cloves.

3. Fill large pot about ¾ full of water. Bring to rolling boil. When boiling, add 1½ tsp. salt. Immediately add broccoli. Cook for 1 minute. Remove broccoli, place in bowl, and set aside.

4. Add fettuccini to boiling water. Stir to separate noodles. Cook according to package directions, until tender yet firm (al denté), at least 15 minutes. When done, drain into colander. In the meantime, reconstitute sun-dried tomatoes by soaking them in ½ c. hot pasta water.

5. Combine beans, nutritional yeast, soymilk, ¾ tsp. salt, turmeric, toasted garlic, and hot pasta water in blender and process until perfectly smooth and silky.

6. Heat blended mixture in wok or very large pot over medium heat. Cut reconstituted sun-dried tomatoes into strips. Stir in cooked broccoli and sun-dried tomatoes. Add drained fettuccini and toss well to coat evenly. Mixture may seem "runny" at first but the pasta will quickly absorb the extra moisture. (After it sits awhile you may even need to add a little more water!)

Bread and Breakfast

Breakfast can be a challenge for those avoiding dairy, eggs, and sugar. This chapter includes a few unsweetened suggestions. Remember, in other cultures it is not uncommon to eat beans, vegetables, rice, soup, and other foods for the first meal of the day. Be adventurous!

All breads and muffins in this book contain no added fats or oils, only the healthy fats that occur naturally in seeds and nuts. Savory breads are a great accompaniment to soups, chili, and stews, or as a basis for snacks and open-faced sandwiches. Try the breads with your choice of any spread in this book. Served warm or toasted, freshly baked bread is the one and only time I recommend real dairy butter as a spread. The sweet dessert breads are best served "naked," not dressed in butter or icing. Baked in mini-loaf pans, they make ideal hostess or holiday gifts. Resist the temptation to slice into hot bread immediately after removing from the oven. Let bread cool for at least 15 minutes before slicing, or it will be "gummy" inside. Be patient!

Whole-Grain Bread (Master Recipe)

Makes 1 loaf

Preparation time: less than 5 minutes

Baking time: varies with type of bread-maker

This dense, hearty, whole-grain bread can be made ONLY in an automatic bread-making machine, as it contains no added fat and is far too sticky to knead by hand. Let the machine do all the work. Experiment with different types of flour and various kinds of sweeteners and additional ingredients. For a slightly lighter loaf, substitute half the flour with unbleached white flour. Always use a serrated knife for slicing bread. Have fun, and happy eating!

4   c. whole-grain flour (recommend
        3 c. stone-ground whole wheat flour
        and 1 c. millet flour)
1   Tbsp. vital wheat gluten
1½ tsp. active dry yeast

2   tsp. sweetener (honey, molasses, maple syrup,
        brown rice syrup, or Sucanat®)
1½ c. soymilk or other non-dairy milk
1   tsp. salt

1. Dump all ingredients (room-temperature) into bread-maker.
2. Turn on automatic bread-maker to whole wheat setting (or equivalent). Wait patiently for at least 3 hours until bread is done.
3. Remove container from bread-maker. Turn upside down on cutting board. Remove bread from container while bread is still a bit warm (it will come out easier). Let it cool about 30 minutes before slicing.

VARIATIONS: Use any whole-grain flours, alone or in combination, to equal 4 c. Try spelt, rye, millet, etc. Add 2 Tbsp. honey, molasses, or other sweetener, if desired. A generous handful of your favorite nuts (walnuts, pecans) or seeds (sunflower, pumpkin, sesame) may be added as well.

Wheat, when milled into white flour, loses a staggering 80% of its nutrients! The so-called "enriched" flour only replaces a tiny fraction of those lost nutrients.

WHOLE WHEAT PASTRY FLOUR VS. REGULAR WHOLE WHEAT FLOUR

Never substitute whole wheat pastry flour for regular whole wheat flour. They are NOT interchangeable. Whole wheat pastry flour is made from a different type of wheat and has a much finer texture, flavor, and baking characteristics. It is so finely textured and neutral in flavor that it can be used instead of white flour in most recipes, but don't try to use whole wheat pastry flour with a bread-maker or to make any yeast-based bread. The finished product will look and taste different because the gluten content is lower. Regular whole wheat flour should only be used for baking yeast-based breads, in my opinion. The best-tasting and most nutritious whole wheat flour is stone-ground. I recommend Bob's Red Mill brand.

Irish Soda Bread (fat-free)

Makes 1 large loaf

Preparation time: 15-20 minutes

Baking time: 50-60 minutes

This simple, hearty quick-bread is the perfect accompaniment to soups and stews. For breakfast or a snack, spread with nut butters or fruit preserves. For a more savory loaf, decrease sweetener and increase salt.

3	c. whole wheat pastry flour	1	tsp. baking soda
1	Tbsp. vital wheat gluten	¼	c. unsweetened plain applesauce
½	tsp. salt	⅓	c. nonfat plain yogurt (soy or dairy)
2	Tbsp. honey or barley malt sweetener	1½	c. water (or more)

1. Preheat oven to 350 degrees. Mix flour, gluten, and salt in large bowl. Combine yogurt, baking soda, applesauce, and honey or barley malt sweetener in large glass and stir well, being careful that mixture does not overflow.
3. Add this foamy mixture to dry ingredients and mix well with wooden spoon. Add water until batter is well mixed. (May need up to 2 c. water; add it gradually and mix well.)
4. Spray or coat large loaf pan with oil. Pour batter into pan. Bake 50 to 60 minutes.
5. Remove from pan while still warm. Let cool at least 15 minutes before slicing.

VARIATION: For a savory loaf, use only 1 tsp. honey and increase salt to 1½ tsp.

Dill Bread (fat-free)

Makes 1 large loaf

Preparation time: 20 minutes

Baking time: 50-60 minutes

For an unusual taste treat, follow standard recipe for Irish Soda Bread, using only 1 tsp. honey or sweetener. Add 1½ tsp. salt, 1 tsp. (or more) dill seed and 1 tsp. dried dill weed to batter. Bake as directed at 350 degrees for 60 minutes. Let cool before slicing. Enjoy with any savory dip or spread in this book, or with Tofu Scramble.

ABOUT VITAL WHEAT GLUTEN

Vital wheat gluten is a natural protein found in wheat. It looks like flour but contains far fewer carbohydrates than regular flour. Sometimes it is called "wheat gluten flour." Vital wheat gluten contains 75 to 80% protein. It is used to improve texture and elasticity of yeast dough. Vital wheat gluten binds moisture, creating moist breads and other yeast based baked goods. Store vital wheat gluten in the refrigerator or freezer to prevent it from becoming rancid.

Corn Bread (fat-free)

Serves 8

Preparation time: 10 minutes

Baking time: 20-25 minutes

Serve warm and drizzled with honey, for a hearty down-home treat that nourishes the body and soothes the soul. If possible, bake corn bread in a cast-iron skillet (8- or 9-inch diameter). Wonderful with chili, lentils, and all bean dishes.

1	c. cornmeal	¼	c. water
1	c. whole wheat pastry flour	1	c. nonfat plain yogurt (dairy or soy)
¾	tsp. salt	1	tsp. baking soda
¼	c. Sucanat® or brown sugar	¼	c. applesauce (natural, unsweetened recommended)
1	Tbsp. Ener-G® egg replacer (under "egg replacer" on p. 184)		

1. Preheat oven to 400 degrees. Mix cornmeal, flour, salt, and Sucanat® or sugar together in large bowl.
2. In small glass, combine Ener-G® egg replacer and water and mix with fork until foamy. (You may substitute 2 eggs or 4 egg whites for Ener-G® egg replacer and water.)
3. In separate medium-size bowl, stir together yogurt, baking soda, and applesauce.
4. Combine all liquids with dry ingredients. Mix thoroughly with wire whisk.
5. Very lightly spray or coat 8- or 9-inch cast-iron skillet or cake pan with canola oil. Don't forget to spray the "walls" as well as the "floor" of the skillet or pan. Pour batter into pan.
6. Bake 20 to 25 minutes until golden-brown. Let rest 10 minutes before cutting. Best eaten warm.

Southwestern Corn Bread

Serves 8

Preparation time: 10 minutes

Baking time: 25 minutes

Here is a simple adaptation to Corn Bread, with a little more texture and kick.

	Corn Bread recipe	½	tsp. chili pepper flakes
¾	c. corn	2	chipotle chilies, chopped

1. Follow directions for Corn Bread. Preheat oven to 400 degrees.
2. Add corn, pepper flakes, and chipotle chilies. Mix thoroughly with a wire whisk.
3. Very lightly spray or coat 8- or 9-inch cast-iron skillet or cake pan with canola oil. Don't forget to spray the "walls" as well as the "floor" of the skillet or pan. Pour batter into pan.
4. Bake 20 to 25 minutes until golden-brown. Let rest 10 minutes before cutting. Best eaten warm.

Corn Muffins

Preparation time: 10 minutes

Serves 8

Baking time: 12 minutes

This simple adaptation to Corn Bread can be made with fine cornmeal or coarse polenta cornmeal.

1. Follow recipe for Corn Bread or Southwestern Corn Bread.
2. Line muffin tins with paper baking cups.
3. Scoop batter into paper baking cups, filling ¾ full (about ¼ c. batter for each muffin).
4. Bake 12 minutes at 400 degrees or until golden brown.

Russian Rye Bread

Preparation time: 5 minutes

Makes 1 small loaf

Baking time: 3 hours, depending on type of bread-maker

This dense, delicious bread can ONLY be made in an automatic bread-maker. Enjoy a thin slice with apricot preserves or honey, or spread with Dijon or whole-grain mustard and slices of Yves meatless deli "meats" (fat-free, soy-based salami, Canadian bacon, bologna, ham, etc.). The loaf is small and cube-shaped, and very heavy.

2	c. rye flour	1½	c. warm water (not hot)
1½	tsp. active dry yeast	¼	c. blackstrap molasses
2	c. whole wheat flour	1	Tbsp. caraway seeds
2	Tbsp. vital wheat gluten	¼	tsp. fennel seeds
1½	tsp. salt		

1. Dump all ingredients (at room temperature) into automatic bread-maker.
2. Turn on bread-maker to whole wheat setting (or equivalent). Close lid and forget about it.
3. When done but still warm, remove container from bread-maker and turn upside down on cutting board. Remove loaf. Wait about 30 minutes before slicing. Enjoy!

Orange-Date Muffins

Serves 12

Preparation time: 7 minutes

Baking time: 25 minutes

Delicious, moist, nutritious, and easy, it's hard to believe these muffins are fat-free! High in fiber and flavor, they taste great on their own, without butter or other spreads. For a gluten-free muffin, replace the flour and oat bran with 1½ cups barley flour. (NOTE: This batter must be baked immediately after mixing, so don't mix it up in advance.)

2	large juicy oranges (about 2 c.)	½	c. oat bran
½	c. date pieces or pitted, chopped dates	¾	c. Sucanat® or brown sugar
¼	c. applesauce	1	tsp. baking soda
1	c. whole wheat pastry flour	1	tsp. baking powder

1. Preheat oven to 375 degrees. Grate zest from 1 orange. (A Microplane works best for this.) Peel oranges, cut them into sections, and remove seeds.
2. In blender, combine and process zest, oranges, dates, and applesauce.
3. In mixing bowl, combine and mix remaining ingredients with wire whisk.

4. Dump blender mixture into bowl with dry ingredients and stir with wire whisk. DO NOT OVERMIX or muffins will become "tough" when baked.
5. Line muffin tins with paper baking cups. Fill each with equal amounts of batter, about ⅓ c. per muffin.
6. Bake for 25 minutes. Enjoy warm or at room temperature, without embellishment.

VARIATIONS: Raisins may be substituted for dates.

Banana Bread

Makes 3 mini-loaves

Preparation time: 20 minutes

Baking time: 45 minutes

The perfect solution for over-ripe bananas, this easy bread is high in potassium and flavor.

2	c. whole wheat pastry flour	4	large ripe bananas
2	tsp. baking powder	1½	tsp. vanilla extract
½	tsp. baking soda	⅓	c. nonfat plain yogurt (soy or dairy)
½	tsp. salt	2	tsp. Ener-G® egg replacer
¾	c. walnuts, chopped	¼	c. cool water
¾	c. Sucanat® (or brown sugar)		

1. Lightly coat or spray 3 mini-loaf pans with oil. Preheat oven to 350 degrees.
2. In large bowl, mix together flour, baking powder, baking soda, salt, and walnuts.
3. In medium bowl, mash or mix together bananas, Sucanat®, vanilla extract, and yogurt with electric mixer or   wire whisk.
4. In small glass, mix together (with fork) Ener-G® egg replacer and ¼ c. cool water. (Note: 1 whole egg or 2 egg whites may be substituted for egg replacer and water.) Add this mixture to banana mixture. Stir.
5. Pour the combined liquid mixtures into dry mixture and stir well with wooden spoon or wire whisk until well mixed. Do not use electric mixture or other electric device or bread may turn out spongy or tough.
6. Pour batter into mini-loaf pans and bake for about 30 minutes or until toothpick comes out clean when inserted into center of loaf.
7. When done, invert pan to remove loaf. Cool for at least 10 minutes before slicing.

Pineapple-Carrot Muffins

Serves 12

Preparation time: 5 minutes

Baking time: 25 minutes

Moist, flavorful and easy, these nutritious muffins can be enjoyed plain or frosted. (NOTE: Never make this batter in advance. Muffins must be baked immediately after batter is mixed.)

1	c. whole wheat pastry flour	⅓	c. raisins
½	c. oat flour	1	c. crushed pineapple
1	tsp. baking powder	⅓	c. carrot, finely grated
1	tsp. baking soda	⅓	c. walnuts, chopped (optional)
¾	c. Sucanat® or brown sugar		

1. Preheat oven to 375 degrees. In mixing bowl, combine dry ingredients and mix well with wire whisk.
2. Add pineapple, carrot, and walnuts. Mix with wire whisk, but DO NOT OVERMIX.
3. Line muffin tins with paper baking cups. Fill cups with equal amounts of batter (about ⅓ c. each).
4. Immediately put in preheated oven and bake for about 25 minutes.

Toasty Oat Bread

Makes 1 large loaf

Preparation time: 15 minutes

Baking time: 35 minutes

This hearty, dense bread tastes even better toasted. Excellent with nut butters, fruit preserves, or any bean-based spread such as hummus. Enjoy with your favorite soup or as a breakfast treat.

2¼	c. whole wheat flour		½	tsp. salt
1	c. oat bran		2	c. plain soymilk or other non-dairy milk
1	c. rolled oats		1	Tbsp. lemon juice or apple cider vinegar
2	tsp. baking powder		1	Tbsp. honey or agave nectar
1	tsp. baking soda			

1. Preheat oven to 375 degrees.
2. In large bowl, mix together all dry ingredients with wire whisk.
3. In small bowl, combine soymilk with lemon juice or vinegar. Let stand about 1 minute, then add honey (may substitute barley malt sweetener, brown rice syrup, or maple syrup) and stir well.
4. Add liquids to large bowl with dry ingredients. Mix well with wire whisk.
5. Lightly spray or coat large loaf pan (5x9-inch) with oil. Pour batter evenly into pan. Bake 35 minutes.
6. Remove from oven. Remove bread from pan when bread is cool enough to handle. Let cool completely before slicing. Do NOT ignore this step!
7. Toast slices to intensify flavor.

Fruited Whole-Grain Bread

Makes 1 loaf

Preparation time: about 5 minutes

Baking time: varies with type of bread-maker

Delicious and satisfying, this hearty bread is perfect with nut butters and jam.

4	c. whole wheat flour		¼	c. honey, molasses, maple syrup, or Sucanat®
1	Tbsp. vital wheat gluten		¾	c. dried fruit (raisins, cranberries, dates, apricots, etc.), chopped
1½	tsp. active dry yeast			
1	tsp. salt		1	tsp. cinnamon
1½	c. soymilk or other non-dairy "milk"		¾	c. walnuts, chopped (optional)

1. Dump all ingredients (room-temperature) into bread-maker. Turn on automatic bread-maker to whole wheat setting (or equivalent). Wait patiently for at least 3 hours until bread is done.
2. Remove container from bread-maker. Turn upside down on cutting board. Remove bread from container while bread is still a bit warm (it will come out easier). Let it cool about 30 minutes before slicing.

Ginger-Pumpkin Loaf

Makes 5 mini-loaves

Preparation time: 20 minutes

Baking time: 45 minutes

Moist, rich-tasting, and bursting with flavor and nutrients, the easy, festive loaf is great for holiday parties or everyday snacks.

1½	c. pumpkin, densely packed	1½	tsp. cinnamon
2	Tbsp. blackstrap molasses	1½	tsp. nutmeg
1¾	c. Sucanat® or brown sugar, densely packed	1½	tsp. baking soda
2	tsp. vanilla extract	2	c. hot water
½	tsp. salt	3½	c. whole wheat pastry flour
1-2	tsp. ground ginger (to your taste)	1-2	Tbsp. turbinado sugar (optional)

1. Lightly spray 5 mini-loaf pans with oil. Preheat oven to 350 degrees.
2. In blender, combine pumpkin, molasses, Sucanat®, vanilla, salt, ginger, cinnamon, and nutmeg. Process briefly until smooth.
3. Pour blended mixture into large bowl. Add baking soda and hot water. Mix with wire whisk.
4. Gradually sprinkle in flour, whisking well to avoid lumping.
5. Divide batter equally, pouring equal amount into each mini-loaf pan. Sprinkle top of each loaf with turbinado sugar (optional, but nice).
6. Bake for about 45 minutes, or until toothpick inserted into center comes out clean.
7. Remove loaves from oven. Let rest about 10 minutes, then remove loaves from pans and cool on wire rack or polyethylene cutting board.
8. When cool, slice and enjoy. Do NOT slice while hot or everything will be a gummy mess.

VARIATION: Add ¾ c. walnuts to batter before adding hot water. Walnuts are an excellent source of Omega-3 fatty acids, a "good" fat that is often missing in the diets of vegetarians.

Blackstrap molasses comes from the third boiling of sugar cane and has the least sugar content. It is a good source of calcium, iron, potassium and magnesium.

MISCELLANEOUS BREAKFAST SUGGESTIONS

Papaya with squeeze of lime

Fresh fruits topped with yogurt (soy or dairy)

Fruit Smoothies

Tofu Scramble

Muesli with Rice Milk, Almond Milk, or Soy Milk

Irish Oats with Cinnamon and Flaxseed Meal

Cooked rolled oats, rolled barley, quinoa, or millet

Buckwheat Pancakes with blueberries or banana

Brown Rice Congee with condiments and fish

Grains and Garlic topped with pumpkin seeds and leftover veggies

Brown Rice Cakes with Almond Butter or Tahini (or any spread from this book)

Rice Tabouli or any dish based on beans and brown rice or other non-wheat whole grains

Nori Burritos

Irish Oats with Cinnamon & Flaxseed Meal
Serves 4-6

Cooking time: 30 minutes

Hearty, easy, and a good source of protein, fiber, and Omega-3 fatty acids, this creamy, satisfying breakfast cereal is well worth the extra time it takes to cook. Cinnamon helps stabilize blood sugar.

1¼	c. steel-cut oats	2-3	Tbsp. flaxseed meal
6	c. cool water	2	bananas, sliced
½	tsp. salt		up to 1 c. berries, any kind
1-2	tsp. cinnamon		maple syrup to taste

1. Measure oats, water, and salt into large pot. Bring to boil. Watch carefully and stir occasionally. Lower heat as soon as mixture starts to boil. Don't let it boil over!! Continue stirring until boiling stops.
2. Cover with lid and simmer on lowest heat for 20 minutes, stirring frequently until most of the water is absorbed and oats are creamy. Sprinkle on generous amount of cinnamon and stir it in just before serving.
3. To serve, scoop cooked oats into bowls and top each serving with 1 to 2 tsp. flaxseed meal. Stir in. Add a little Almond Milk, rice milk, soymilk, or other nondairy milk. (Note: Flaxseed meal adds fiber, Omega-3 fatty acids, and other nutrients. It also acts as a thickener because it absorbs liquid. If needed, more nondairy milk may be added to cereal just before serving.)
4. Top with slices of banana and berries, and a very light drizzle of maple syrup.

Muesli

Serves 8-10

Preparation time: 5-10 minutes

Great for a quick breakfast, this muesli provides fiber, calcium, Vitamin E, protein, Omega-3 fatty acids, and lots of energy. Make a large batch and keep it refrigerated.

½	c. raw pumpkin seeds, shelled		½	c. dried cranberries
6	c. quick-cooking rolled oats		1	c. dried apricots, chopped
½	c. oat bran		½	c. dates, chopped (optional)
½	c. almonds, slivered or sliced		½	c. flaxseed meal
¼	c. raw sunflower seeds, shelled		¾	c. powdered soymilk
1	c. raisins			

1. Scoop raw pumpkin seeds into large skillet and heat until seeds start popping and getting puffy. Add rolled oats and oat bran.
2. Add rolled oats, oat bran, sunflower seeds, and almonds. Stir constantly over medium heat until oats smell "toasty," about 5 minutes. Do not allow to brown!
3. Add raisins, dried cranberries, apricots, and dates. Stir to combine.
4. Remove from heat. Let cool completely. To fortify with added protein and calcium, add powdered soymilk. ("Better than Milk" is a good brand.) Add flaxseed meal and stir well.
5. When thoroughly cooled to room temperature, store in Ziploc bags or tightly sealed jar or container.

TO SERVE COLD: Scoop about 1 c. muesli into each bowl. Mix with good-quality plain yogurt or generous amounts of non-dairy milk (soy, rice, almond, oat, etc.). For a chewy texture, serve immediately. For a soft, mushy texture, use more liquid and wait a few minutes before eating. Top with your favorite fresh fruits. Enjoy!

VARIATION: Add different chopped nuts (not peanuts or cashews), chopped dried fruits, or a dash of cinnamon.

TRAVELING TIP

Muesli is the perfect food for traveling. Pack it in Ziploc freezer bags and keep a supply on hand for breakfast or snacking anytime, anywhere. Just add water and the muesli makes its own "milk" because of the powdered soymilk in the mix. It can be eaten hot or cold and is a soothing "comfort food." Muesli does not require refrigeration when stored in Ziploc freezer bags or other tightly sealed containers.

> ### INSTANT HOT CEREAL
>
> Scoop about 1 cup Muesli into each bowl. Pour about 1½ cups boiling water over muesli and stir. Let sit about 2 minutes. Honey, Sucanat®, or brown sugar may be added to taste. Add a little Almond Milk, soymilk, or other milk, if desired. (Note: Muesli is highly absorbent; you may need to add more liquid than you think.)

Instant Almond Milk (cereal version)   Serves 3-4

Preparation time: 2 minutes or less

A high-speed blender makes this nutritious nondairy milk substitute in a flash. Make only what you can drink in 24 hours. Best if chilled, unless serving over hot cereal. For finer, whiter "milk," use blanched or hot-soaked almonds (see Beverages & Frozen Treats section).

½ c. raw almonds	up to 1 c. crushed ice (optional)
2 c. filtered cold water	

1. Toss raw almonds into blender. Add water. Cover tightly and process on high until almonds are pulverized. If using milk with cold cereal, add crushed ice and blend on high until ice dissolves.
2. Pour directly over cereal and enjoy! The almond sediment adds texture, flavor, and nutrition to your cereal. For use as a drink, filter almond milk through fine-meshed sieve. Use the thick, creamy sediment as a topping for creamy soups. Consistency of sediment depends on speed of blender and amount of time beverage is blended.

(Note: Use more almonds and/or less water for thicker "milk." Add more ice cubes for colder "milk." Store tightly covered in refrigerator and use within 2 days.)

Oatcakes (fat-free)   Serves 10-12

Preparation time: 20 minutes   Baking time: 60 minutes

These hearty date-filled "hockey pucks" are easy to make and taste wonderful, although they are virtually fat-free. The dates add moisture and produce a chewy texture, especially when oatcakes are warm. Use a ½ cup straight-sided measuring cup as a mold to form oatcakes. For diabetics or people with sugar sensitivity, use brown rice syrup OR barley malt sweetener in place of brown sugar. It works just as well and tastes good. The secret to the success of these oatcakes is to bake them at very low heat.

4½	c. rolled oats	
1½	c. whole wheat pastry flour	
½	c. brown sugar, firmly packed	
2	tsp. baking powder	
¼	tsp. salt	

⅓	c. nonfat plain yogurt (soy or dairy)
⅓	c. applesauce
⅓	c. water
1	c. date pieces
2-3	Tbsp. rolled oats

1. In mixing bowl, combine oats, flour, brown sugar, baking powder, and salt.
2. Add yogurt, applesauce, water, and dates. Mix well with electric mixer.
3. Preheat oven to 225 degrees. Line baking sheet with parchment.
4. Sprinkle about ½ tsp. rolled oats in bottom of ½-c. mold (about 3 inch diameter and 1¼ inches high). Do NOT skip this step or dough will be impossible to unmold! Press dough firmly into mold. Unmold onto parchment. Repeat until all dough is gone.
5. Bake for 60 minutes. Enjoy warm or at room temperature. Store remainder in Ziploc plastic bag in refrigerator. Reheat chilled oatcakes in microwave to perk up flavor, soften dates, and create a tempting aroma.

Buckwheat Pancake Mix

Makes 4 ½ cups mix

Preparation time: 5 minutes

This pancake mix is sugar-free, egg-free, and oil-free. These pancakes are far more nutritious than ordinary pancakes, and amazingly, they taste great! You won't have to toss out the first pancake, because these pancakes always turn out right—IF you use a good quality nonstick skillet. Double this pancake mix recipe and keep the mix on hand for a quick, convenient, easy family breakfast.

⅓	c. raw wheat germ
1	c. oat bran
⅓	c. flaxseeds
1	Tbsp. baking powder

1⅓	c. buckwheat flour
1⅓	c. whole wheat pastry flour
⅓	c. vital wheat gluten
1	tsp. salt

1. Combine wheat germ, oat bran, and flaxseeds in blender and process thoroughly, at least 30 seconds or until flaxseeds are ground up.
2. Dump blender mixture into large bowl and add baking powder, flours, gluten, and salt. Mix everything well with wire whisk or electric mixer.
3. Store pancake mix in Ziploc freezer bag or large glass jar with tight-seal lid. Refrigerate until ready to use.

Quick Buckwheat Pancakes (from mix) Makes 12 (6-inch) pancakes

Preparation time: 2 minutes   Cooking time: depends on size of griddle or skillet

Easy, hearty, and good for you, these pancakes can be made in a flash using the basic Buckwheat Pancake Mix. Keep the mix on hand and you will make pancakes more often. Your family will thank you!

3	c. Buckwheat Pancake Mix	1	tsp. baking soda
½	c. nonfat plain yogurt (soy or dairy)	3	c. water or soymilk (or other non-dairy milk)
¼	c. applesauce		

1. In large mixing bowl, mix together pancake mix, yogurt, applesauce, and baking soda.
2. Add water or soymilk. Mix with wire whisk until just combined. Batter will thicken if it sits for even a couple of minutes, so stir in a little more liquid as needed.
3. Heat good-quality nonstick skillet or griddle. (No need to use oil.) Use ¼ c. batter for each pancake. (For larger pancakes use ⅓ c. batter.) Turn heat down to medium. When bubbles start to appear on surface of pancake, carefully flip pancake. Do not press down or flip again! Serve immediately with Maple-Flaxseed Oil Syrup.

Blueberry-Buckwheat Pancakes (from mix)

Makes 12 (6-inch) pancakes

Preparation time: 2 minutes   Cooking time: depends on size of griddle or skillet

A delicious variation, the blueberries provide antioxidants and flavor.

3	c. Buckwheat Pancake Mix	3	c. water or soymilk (or other non-dairy milk)
½	c. nonfat plain yogurt (soy or dairy)		up to 2 c. whole blueberries (fresh or frozen)
¼	c. applesauce	1½	c. Almond Cream (optional)
1	tsp. baking soda		

1. In large mixing bowl, mix together pancake mix, yogurt, applesauce, and baking soda.
2. Add water or soymilk. Mix with wire whisk until just combined. Batter will thicken if it sits for even a couple of minutes, so stir in a little more liquid, as needed.
3. Heat good-quality nonstick skillet or griddle. (No need to use oil.) Use ¼ c. batter for each pancake. (For larger pancakes use ⅓ c. batter.) Turn heat down to medium. Scatter blueberries on surface of pancake (they will sink into the batter while pancake is cooking). When bubbles start to appear on surface of pancake, carefully flip it. Do not press down or flip again!

4. Serve immediately with maple syrup, more blueberries, or Maple-Flaxseed Oil Pancake Syrup. For a dessert-like pancake, top with fresh blueberries and dollop of Almond Cream (see Beverages & Frozen Treats).

Maple-Flaxseed Oil Syrup
Makes 1½ cups

Preparation time: 30 seconds

Flaxseed oil provides Omega-3 fatty acids and a rich buttery texture. Combined with good quality pure maple syrup, this makes a healthful, satisfying substitute for butter and commercial pancake syrup.

1 c. maple syrup (the real thing, Grade B preferred)
½ c. Barlean's flaxseed oil (shake well before using)

1. In bottle with tight-fitting lid, combine maple syrup and flaxseed oil. Screw lid on very tightly. Shake very well to combine. Pour over pancakes or waffles instead of butter or other syrup.
2. Store remainder in refrigerator and use within 2 weeks. Always shake well before using!

Banana-Buckwheat Pancakes (from mix)
Makes 12 (6-inch) pancakes

Preparation time: 2 minutes   Cooking time: depends on size of griddle or skillet

When the bananas are ripening all at the same time, make these pancakes. Yum!

3 c. Buckwheat Pancake Mix
½ c. nonfat plain yogurt (soy or dairy)
¼ c. applesauce
1 tsp. baking soda

3 c. water or soymilk (or other non-dairy milk)
3 bananas, diced
2 bananas, sliced
1½ c. Almond Cream (optional)

1. In large mixing bowl, mix together pancake mix, yogurt, applesauce, and baking soda.
2. Add water or soymilk. Mix with wire whisk until just combined. Add diced bananas and gently stir with wooden spoon. Batter will thicken if it sits for even a couple of minutes, so stir in a little more liquid, as needed.
3. Heat good-quality nonstick skillet or griddle. (No need to use oil.) Use ¼ c. batter for each pancake. (For larger pancakes use ⅓ c. batter.) Turn heat down to medium. When bubbles start to appear on surface of pancake, carefully flip pancake. Do not press down or flip again!
4. Serve immediately with maple syrup or Maple-Flaxseed Oil Pancake Syrup. For a dessert-like treat, top with sliced bananas and dollop of Almond Cream. (Note: Use perfectly ripe bananas that are not dark brown and mushy.)

Tofu Scramble

Preparation time: 5 minutes

1 block tofu serves 2-3

Cooking time: 5 minutes

Ideal for a quick breakfast or dressed up for lunch, Tofu Scramble can be made with any kind of firm or extra-firm tofu. Fresh vegetables and herbs create a festive, colorful dish that may be eaten warm or at room temperature. Tofu Scramble makes a tasty mock "egg" salad or pita stuffing.

- 1   block (16-20 oz.) tofu
- 2   Tbsp. nutritional yeast flakes
- ¼   tsp. turmeric (or less)
- ¼   tsp. salt
  pepper (a few grinds)
- 2   Tbsp. diced bell pepper (any color)
- 2   Tbsp. diced tomato
- 2   Tbsp. fresh herbs (dill, scallions, chives, basil, tarragon, your choice)
- 1-2 Tbsp. diced purple onion (optional)
  few drops extra virgin olive oil (to finish)

142

1. Cut block of tofu in half and wrap tightly in cotton tea-towel until towel is saturated. In nonstick skillet, mash or crumble drained tofu. Add salt, yeast flakes, turmeric, and freshly ground pepper and mix well with fork. Scramble mixture with spatula over medium heat until bright yellow and heated through.
2. Stir in your choice of vegetables and herbs, singly or in any combination. Add a few drops of good olive oil just before serving. Adjust seasoning to taste.

Brown Rice Congee
Serves 2-3

Cooking time: overnight

This soupy, fortifying Chinese porridge is easy to digest and very versatile. Start cooking congee before you go to bed and it will be ready to eat when you wake up.

¼   c. short-grain brown rice
4   c. water
¼   tsp. salt

1. In medium pot, combine rice, water, and salt. Cover pot and bring to boil. Reduce heat to lowest setting. Simmer 4 to 6 hours or overnight.
2. Serve in bowls topped with chopped scallions, crumbled nori (seaweed) and sesame seeds. Add a dash of Bragg Liquid Aminos for flavor.
3. On the side or as toppings, serve congee with your choice(s) of condiments such as:

cooked vegetables	sunflower seeds
pumpkins seeds	cooked beans (any kind)
cilantro	green onion, chopped

Millet Congee

A simple variation on Brown Rice Congee, Millet Congee is definitely not just bird seed!

Follow the above recipe exactly, substituting millet instead of brown rice. Enjoy!

Quinoa Congee

Cook quinoa following procedure for Brown Rice Congee, substituting quinoa for rice. When cooked, tiny white spirals form on quinoa. Quinoa provides substantial protein and a unique nutty flavor to any dish. Quinoa MUST be thoroughly rinsed before cooking to remove its bitter outer coating.

Beverages and Frozen Treats

The following recipes require no added sweetener of any kind, yet they are exquisitely flavored and sweet enough to satisfy anyone. The secrets are in the fruits (fresh, frozen, or dried) and good-quality extracts. A high-speed blender is all you need to create your own nutritious, delicious, inexpensive nondairy "milk" beverages, smoothies, sorbets, and Popsicles. Milk substitute can be made for only pennies a quart, and the time it takes to make it is about the same as the time it takes to open a carton of milk. You can make it fresh every day, or make extra and store in the refrigerator for up to 3 days. Any of these "milk" recipes can be used as the basis for smoothies, sorbets, Popsicles, puddings, or baked goods. This "milk" is ideal for pouring over breakfast cereal, or enjoying chilled on its own (or with cookies). It even makes a great hot beverage, flavored with a dash of vanilla or almond extract.

Oat Milk

Yield: 3+ cups

Preparation time: 2 minutes or less

You may never buy nondairy milk substitutes again after making your own. With a high-speed blender, nutritious, delicious drinks can be made fresh for only pennies (less than 5 cents) a serving.

¾ c. rolled oats
3 c. filtered water
2 pitted dates

1-2 tsp. light agave nectar or maple syrup (optional)
1 tsp. almond extract

1. Toss rolled oats (any kind, whatever is cheapest) into blender. Process on high speed until oats turn into fine flour (varies according to type of blender).
2. Add filtered water (do not use tap water unless it is pure and tastes good), agave nectar, dates, and almond extract. Blend on high, holding lid down tightly, until dates are pulverized.
3. Use in shakes, smoothies, and frozen treats. Pour over cereal or simply enjoy as a beverage. Store remainder in glass jar with tight seal and use within 3 days.

VARIATION: Use vanilla extract or other flavoring instead of almond extract.

Almond Milk

Serves 4-6

Preparation time: 2 minutes plus soak time   Soak time: 15 minutes or overnight

Soaking almonds makes them easier to blend and easier to digest. Soaking them gets rid of the tannins that cause bitterness, which is why soaked almonds taste slightly "sweet." Soaking also releases the enzyme inhibitors and allows the almonds to begin sprouting, which increases their nutritional value and digestibility. Almonds are a good source of protein and calcium.

¼ - ½ c. soaked almonds (see p.146)
1 c. plus 2 c. filtered cold water

up to 1 c. crushed ice (optional)
1-2 tsp. agave nectar, to taste (optional)

1. Put soaked almonds in high-speed blender. Add 1 c. water. Blend at high speed until almonds are ground up very finely. (Time varies with type of blender used.)
2. Add up to 2 c. cold water (the amount of water depends on how rich you like your milk). For ice-cold almond milk, add up to 1 c. crushed ice before final blending. Blend until ice dissolves. For sweeter almond milk, add agave nectar before final blending. If perfectly smooth milk is required, pour almond milk through a fine-mesh strainer or cheesecloth.
3. Store in glass jar and cover with tight-fitting lid. Refrigerate immediately and use within 2 days. (Note: Almond milk will separate and requires shaking before every use.)

145

HOW TO SOAK ALMONDS

Pour 1 cup raw almonds into a quart-size mixing bowl. Run the tap until the water gets very hot. Cover the almonds with the hot tap water, allowing at least 1 inch of head room. Wait until the water gets cool enough to touch. Swish the water and almonds. (The water will become reddish-brown.) Drain the water, rinse the almonds, and dump the almonds back into the bowl. Run fresh cool water over the almonds. Soak almonds overnight for best results. (The longer the almonds soak, the larger they swell and the easier they are to blend.) To store for later use, put the soaked almonds in a glass jar. Cover with fresh cold water, and seal with a tight-fitting lid. Refrigerate and use within 5 days.

Almond Cream

Preparation time: 2 minutes or less

The perfect topping for desserts, this is an adaptation of Almond Milk using blanched almonds.

½	c. blanched almonds (see below)	1	tsp. agave nectar
¾	c. filtered ice water	¼	tsp. almond extract

1. Toss blanched almonds into blender. Add filtered ice water, agave nectar, and almond extract. Cover tightly and blend until almonds are pulverized and product is the consistency of thick cream.
2. Scoop on top of your favorite desserts or drinks, as a substitute for whipped cream. For thicker Almond Cream, use more almonds.

HOW TO BLANCH ALMONDS

To blanch almonds (remove the skins), immerse almonds in boiling water for about 5 minutes. Remove almonds from boiling water and submerge them in ice water. Swish. Skins should slip off easily. This also gets rid of some of the bitter tannins. Remove almonds from water and use in your favorite recipes. Discard skins.

Cashew Milk

Yield: 3+ cups

Preparation time: 2 minutes

An excellent, simple, inexpensive, good-tasting way to make your own "instant" milk substitute for cereals and smoothies, and something fun to drink when you eat cookies.

¾ c. cashews

2 c. plus 2 c. filtered cold water

1-2 tsp. maple syrup or agave nectar (optional)

1-2 tsp. almond extract or vanilla extract (optional)

1. Toss cashews into blender and process on high speed grind until product becomes like "flour" or fine meal.
2. Add 2 c. filtered water. Blend on high, holding lid securely, until mixture is smooth. Add remaining 2 c. water and blend again. If sweeter milk is preferred, add maple syrup or agave nectar. Almond extract or vanilla extract may be added before second blending.
3. Strain through several layers of cheesecloth or a mesh bag if smoother texture is required. Do not strain if using for cereal or smoothies. Store in glass jar with tight seal and use within 3 days.

THE BEST ALL-PURPOSE KITCHEN APPLIANCE EVER!

My favorite kitchen appliance is the Blendtec® Champ HP3 by K-Tec, the all-purpose high-performance blender/grinder/crusher/processor that is used commercially by many well-known food and beverage establishments. It is well worth the price, and the warranty is unbeatable. You may actually "retire" your juicer, food processor, coffee grinder, blender, food mill, and ice crusher. The Blendtec® Champ HP3 does a better job—and much faster, with no assembly and virtually no cleanup required. I have tried (and owned) "comparable" products manufactured by this company's main competitors, and believe me, there is NO comparison, regardless of price. So take it from someone who learned the hard way...and now has a cupboard full of expensive, well-known, popular kitchen appliances that she may never again need to use. By the way, if you can't afford the Blendtec® Champ HP3 at this time, make do with any blender. It will take a lot longer and the results will not be optimal, but it will be workable.

Basic Fruit Smoothies (Master Recipe)   Makes 8 cups, serves 4-6

Preparation time: about 5 minutes, depends on type of fruit and type of blender

This recipe makes a blender-full, enough for several smoothies with some left over to make some Popsicles. Experiment with whatever fruits are available. Fresh or frozen work equally well, but the bananas must be frozen to achieve the perfect texture. To make Popsicles, simply pour the remainder into Popsicle molds and freeze until solid, about 4 hours.

up to 2 c. soymilk (or other non-dairy milk)

⅔   c. nonfat plain yogurt (6 oz. container)

½   c. frozen orange juice concentrate

1-2   c. berries, peaches, or other fruit (fresh or frozen)

2   large or 3 small frozen bananas, cut into 1-inch chunks

handful ice cubes (optional)

1. Put all ingredients in blender, starting with soft and liquid ingredients on bottom and ending with frozen fruits and ice on top. Blend until smooth. (Note: If using a standard blender, you may need to start and stop several times, tamping down the fruit and ice very carefully.)
2. Pour blended mixture into glasses and enjoy! Pour any remaining into Popsicle molds and freeze until solid to enjoy later.

VARIATIONS: Add ¼ c. soy or whey protein powder or 3 oz. silken Lite tofu for added protein. More fruits may be added, according to personal preference. Pure organic fruit juice may be substituted for part of the milk.

Basic Fruit Sorbet

Preparation time: 5-10 minutes, depends on type of fruit and type of blender

Use whatever fruits are available, in whatever amounts you prefer. Place soft ingredients first in bottom of blender and frozen fruits and ice cubes last. Follow master recipe (Basic Fruit Smoothies), using only 1 c. soymilk and more ice cubes. If desired, substitute part or all of the soymilk with fruit juice (not fruit "drink"). Blend until sorbet-like texture is achieved. This may require stopping and starting blender several times, tamping down fruit and ice when blender is stopped. Do NOT tamp when blender is operating, or disaster may result!!

HOW TO FREEZE BANANAS

Frozen bananas are the secret to these creamy smoothies and desserts. Choose bananas that are perfectly ripe, with no green at all and with no soft brown spots. Carefully peel, making sure to remove all the "strings." Cut in half and place in quart-size Ziploc plastic freezer bags. Seal bag and freeze immediately. Remove only the amount needed for a recipe and return the bag of bananas to the freezer immediately. (These recipes will NOT work with unfrozen or thawed bananas). Bananas all seem to ripen at the same time, and this is a great way to use them without feeling obligated to bake banana bread. They keep almost indefinitely if frozen in a tightly sealed plastic freezer bag. Frozen bananas impart an exceptional creamy texture that cannot be duplicated. Never attempt these recipes with fresh bananas or mashed bananas.

Blueberry-Banana Smoothies   Serves 4-5

Preparation time: about 5 minutes, depends on type of blender

Blueberries are a superior source of antioxidants and bananas are high in potassium, which makes this an excellent smoothie or dessert for anyone.

Follow master recipe (Basic Fruit Smoothies), using up to 2 c. blueberries (fresh or frozen) as the fruit. If desired, use vanilla-flavored soymilk and berry-flavored yogurt instead of plain. Blend on high for longer than usual, because blueberry skins are tough and it takes a while to achieve a smooth texture. When smooth, pour into tall glasses and freeze the remainder in Popsicle molds.

Power Smoothies   Serves 4-5

Preparation time: depends on type of blender and types of fruits

These tasty high-protein smoothies are also high in Omega-3s and fiber.

Basic Fruit Smoothies (Master Recipe)	½ c. protein powder (soy, rice, or whey)
½ c. raw macadamia nuts or almonds	2 Tbsp. flaxseed meal

Prepare master recipe (Basic Fruit Smoothies), using any assortment of fresh or frozen fruit. Add raw nuts, protein powder, and flaxseed meal. Blend on high until nuts are ground up to desired consistency. (Note: Flaxseed is highly absorbent, so mixture may thicken before ready to serve. If needed, add more non-dairy milk and blend to desired consistency.)

149

Ice Dream

Preparation time: 5 minutes, if bananas are already frozen and equipment is set up

This simple dessert requires special equipment: a Champion juicer (no other type of juicer will work), or a high performance blender such as K-Tec HP3 Champ. Bananas must be rock solid and Ice Dream must be eaten immediately.

1   large frozen banana per serving

⅓   c. frozen berries or other frozen fruits (optional)

1. Allowing 1 large frozen banana per serving, process frozen bananas (see How to Freeze Bananas) until creamy but not mushy.
2. Serve immediately. Enjoy in a bowl like ice cream or as topping for fruit crisps and pies "à la mode".

Strawberry Ice Dream Pie
Serves 8

Preparation time: 10 minutes   Freeze time: at least 2 hours   Thaw time: 20-30 minutes

A no-bake, dairy-free dessert that can be made ahead. Don't forget to take it out of the freezer about 20 minutes before serving.

3   perfectly ripe bananas (about 2 c.), cut into chunks

1   tsp. fresh lemon juice (not bottled)

8-10 oz. silken Lite tofu, firm or extra-firm (about ¾ box)

¾   c. strawberry purée (or use ½ box frozen strawberries)

1   tsp. almond extract

graham cracker crust

berries and mint for garnish

1. Combine bananas, lemon juice, tofu, and strawberry purée in blender. Process until very smooth and creamy.
2. Pour blended mixture into graham cracker crust (buy pre-made or make your own). Smooth top. Freeze until solid, at least 2 hours. (Note: If there is too much filling for 1 pie, pour remainder into Popsicle molds or make Strawberry Ice Dream Sandwiches and freeze to enjoy later.)
3. Remove from freezer 20 to 30 minutes before serving, to allow pie to thaw slightly. Garnish with berries and mint, if desired. After 20 minutes, try to slice the pie. If pie is still frozen solid, wait a few more minutes and try again. Serve as soon as it is thawed enough to slice.
4. Wrap remaining pie in plastic cling wrap and refreeze immediately.

Strawberry Ice Dream Tarts

Makes 24 tarts

Preparation time: 10 minutes or less   Freeze time: 1 hour   Thaw time: 10 minutes or less

These tarts aren't really tart, they are individual-size Ice Dream Pies and we couldn't think of what else to call them. Best if eaten with a fork.

Strawberry Ice Dream Pie Recipe

24   fat-free vanilla wafers (Frookies brand recommended)

6   strawberries, sliced into "hearts" (optional)

1. Prepare Strawberry Ice Dream Pie according to recipe.
2. Place 24 baking cups in muffin tins. Place vanilla wafer in each.
3. Scoop or pour 2 Tbsp. pie mixture into each baking cup. Top each with a strawberry slice.
4. Freeze until solid, at least 1 hour. Remove from freezer 5 minutes before serving. Eat immediately.

Strawberry Ice Dream Sandwiches

Makes 24 small treats

Preparation time: 10 minutes or less   Freeze time: 1 hour   Thaw time: 10 minutes or less

A fun, fat-free, strawberry mini-version of ice cream sandwiches.

Strawberry Ice Dream Pie recipe
48   fat-free vanilla wafers (Frookies brand
          recommended)

1. Prepare Strawberry Ice Dream Tarts according to recipe. Top each tart with another vanilla wafer.
2. Freeze until solid, for at least 1 hour. Remove from freezer 5 minutes before serving. Peel off paper baking cup and enjoy immediately.

Banana-Berry Sorbet

Serves 4

Preparation time: 5 minutes

This simple sorbet requires only three ingredients. It may be made using a high-performance blender or food-processor. Make it immediately before serving.

about 10 oz. frozen mixed berries
2-3   large frozen bananas, cut into 1-inch chunks
¼   c. non-dairy milk, berry juice, or cherry juice

1. Combine all ingredients in blender.
2. Process until blended and smooth. For an icier dessert, add ½ c. crushed ice to blender. (Depending on type of blender, this may require stopping and starting a couple of times, tamping down frozen ingredients when blender is stopped. Be careful!)

VARIATION: Experiment with different kinds of berries, singly or in combination. Blackberries and raspberries are good choices. Frozen strawberries need to be cut into chunks before blending. Frozen peaches or nectarines work well too. Add extra berries or bananas, if desired (proportions do not need to be exact).

Frozen Pops ("Popsicles")

You won't believe how easy it is to make your own frozen treats on a stick—Popsicles—that taste great and are good for you!

Simply make your favorite smoothie or fruit-based beverage. Pour remainder into Popsicle molds (available at kitchen specialty shops). Each Popsicle mold holds about ½ c. These are so delicious and healthful that we recommend you eat them for breakfast on a hot summer day. The beauty of these treats is that none of them contain refined sugar in any form, yet they are all tantalizingly sweet. The sweetness comes entirely from the fruit.

ABOUT SOYMILK

Before you decide you don't like soymilk, try several varieties. Soymilk comes in low-fat, creamy, fortified, flavored (vanilla and chocolate are most common), high-sugar, low-sugar, delicious, and just plain yucky. Each one tastes different. Read the labels carefully, and select the brand and type of soymilk based on its intended use (over cereal, baking sweets, in smoothies, for gravies, and soups). For gravies, sauces, and soups, select soymilk with no added sweeteners. Even "plain" soymilks vary tremendously in the amount of sugar they contain. For example, Vitasoy Creamy Original has only 4 grams of sugar per serving, as compared to other brands of plain soymilk with as many as 14 grams(!) of sugar per serving. (Obviously, a sweet soymilk will ruin a savory sauce.) I prefer to make my own non-dairy milks from scratch.

FruiTeasers (fruit juice and herbal tea delights)

Preparation time: 15 minutes

Hot or cold, liquid or frozen, FruiTeasers adapt to accommodate huge crowds and varied tastes. If there is any left over, just pour into Popsicle molds and enjoy as a cool treat later.

1. Brew a pot of your favorite herbal tea. Make it strong.
2. Combine with equal amount of fruit juice (most fruits work well, but avoid grapefruit or prune juice).
3. Serve iced in tall glasses, garnished with a wedge of lemon or orange, or a sprig of mint. If making for a crowd, serve in punchbowl with an ice ring, garnished with floating lemon slices. For a carbonated beverage, add a little ginger ale.

VARIATION: To serve hot, simmer fruit juice and steeped tea in large pot Serve in mugs with cinnamon sticks. Pour remaining (cooled) beverage into Popsicle molds and freeze.

Apple-Zinger Hot Cider

Serves a large crowd

Preparation time: 10-15 minutes

Refreshingly "zingy" yet pleasantly sweet, this beverage contains no refined sugar or added sweetener of any kind. The possibilities are limited only by your imagination. Serve hot or iced.

CHOOSE ONE TEA:	Cinnamon Apple Spice	Red Zinger	Lemon Zinger
	Wild Berry Zinger	Cranberry Apple Zinger	Honey Peach Ginger

2 quarts organic apple juice
cinnamon sticks (optional)

1. Fill teakettle with water and bring to rolling boil. In large teapot, place 4 tea bags. Choose 1 of the teas above, or similar. (Note: Celestial Seasonings brand makes excellent herbal teas.) Pour boiling water over tea bags, cover, and let steep for 10 to 15 minutes or longer.
2. Meanwhile, pour apple juice into large pot or Dutch oven. (Fill almost halfway.) Turn heat on low.
3. Add steeped tea to apple juice. Mix. Serve hot in mugs, with cinnamon sticks.

Apple-Zinger Punch

Serves a crowd

Preparation time: 10-15 minutes

An iced version of Apple-Zinger Hot Cider, this refreshing punch looks fabulous if served in a punchbowl with an ice ring floating in it. Simply pour herbal tea or apple juice into a Bundt pan or other ring-shaped mold, filling halfway to allow for expansion during freezing. Freeze a day or two ahead of time. An ice ring keeps the punch chilled without watering it down. If you don't have an ice ring, use ice cubes.

1. Brew your choice of herbal tea according to Apple-Zinger Hot Cider recipe.
2. Place ice ring in punchbowl. Pour apple juice over ice ring, filling punchbowl halfway.
3. Pour steeped tea into punchbowl, filling to about 2 inches from rim of bowl. Garnish with lemon slices, if desired.

VARIATION: For a carbonated punch, substitute ginger ale for part of the tea or apple juice. Freeze any remaining punch in Popsicle molds to enjoy later.

Tropical Smoothies

Serves 4-5

Preparation time: depends on type of blender and types of fruits

Perfect during mango season or when tropical fruits are plentiful, this smoothie works equally well with fresh or frozen fruit. When faced with an overabundance of mangoes or other fruits, simply freeze in 1 or 2 cup portions in Ziploc freezer bags. An excellent source of beta-carotene and vitamin C, tropical fruits combine well with other fruits for an unusual, exotic smoothie or frozen dessert.

1½ c. soymilk (or any other non-dairy milk)	¼-inch slice lime, including peel
⅔ c. nonfat plain yogurt (6 oz. container)	(cut lime slice like a wheel)
½ c. frozen orange juice concentrate (with calcium)	2 small frozen bananas, cut into 1-inch chunks
1-2 c. mango (fresh or frozen), peeled and chopped	⅓ c. pineapple, chunks or crushed (optional)
	handful ice cubes (optional)

1. Prepare master recipe (Basic Fruit Smoothies), using fresh or frozen mango as the main fruit. Add a ¼-inch slice lime (including peel).
2. If desired, toss in a few chunks of pineapple. Amount of soymilk may be decreased or substituted in part with pineapple juice, if desired.
3. Blend on high speed until lime peel is finely ground up, with no chunky green bits floating around.
4. Pour into tall glasses and garnish with a wedge of pineapple or lime. Pour remainder into Popsicle molds and freeze until solid.

More mangoes are eaten fresh all over the world than any other fruit.

Tropical Sorbet

Serves 4

Preparation time: depends on type of blender and types of fruits

For a sorbet-style dessert, use half the amount of liquid and add extra ice-cubes to Tropical Smoothie mixture before blending. Blend until sorbet-like texture is achieved. This may require stopping and starting the blender several times, tamping down ice and frozen fruits when blender has stopped. Do not tamp when blender is operating, or disaster may result.

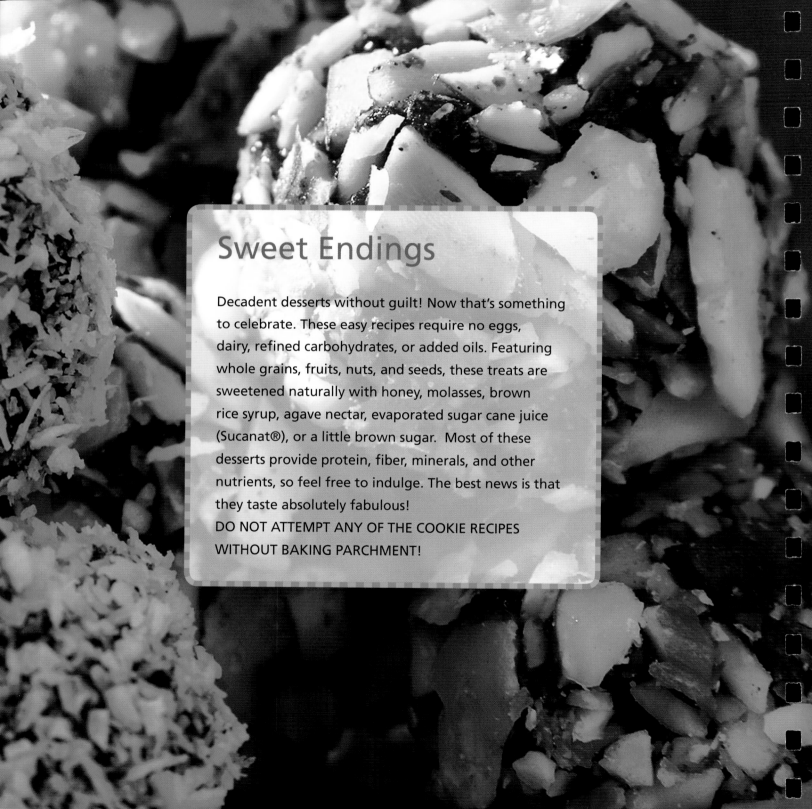

Sweet Endings

Decadent desserts without guilt! Now that's something to celebrate. These easy recipes require no eggs, dairy, refined carbohydrates, or added oils. Featuring whole grains, fruits, nuts, and seeds, these treats are sweetened naturally with honey, molasses, brown rice syrup, agave nectar, evaporated sugar cane juice (Sucanat®), or a little brown sugar. Most of these desserts provide protein, fiber, minerals, and other nutrients, so feel free to indulge. The best news is that they taste absolutely fabulous!

DO NOT ATTEMPT ANY OF THE COOKIE RECIPES
WITHOUT BAKING PARCHMENT!

Oatmeal-Date Nuggets (fat-free)

Makes 24-30 cookies

Preparation time: 15 minutes

Baking time: 10-12 minutes

These chewy morsels are rich in fiber and flavor. Low oven temperature prevents the cookies from drying out or burning. Prune purée replaces butter and eggs and yields a moist, nutritious cookie. Date pieces are available in bulk in many health food stores. They look like tiny cylinders and are dusted with oat flour. If you can't find them, just use finely chopped dates. Enjoy!

½	c. Sucanat® or brown sugar, firmly packed	¼	tsp. salt
⅓	c. prune purée	2	tsp. cinnamon or pumpkin pie spice (or 1 tsp. each)
1	tsp. vanilla extract OR maple flavoring	¼	c. soymilk (or other nondairy milk)
¾	c. whole wheat pastry flour (see note)	1½	c. rolled oats
½	tsp. baking soda	¼	c. oat bran
¼	tsp. baking powder	½	c. date pieces or chopped dates

1. Preheat oven to 300 degrees. Combine first 9 ingredients (everything except rolled oats, oat bran and dates) in large bowl and mix until smooth, using electric mixer.
2. Add remaining ingredients and mix thoroughly with wooden spoon or electric mixer.
3. Line cookie sheet with baking parchment. Drop dough by spoonful, using 2 spoons—1 to scoop, and 1 to scrape dough onto parchment-lined cookie sheet. (Dough "blobs" should be almost the size of a golf ball.) Do not try to form balls with your hands. The dough is too sticky and it won't work.
4. Bake 10 to 12 minutes. Remove cookies from oven and lightly press each 1 to flatten, if desired (use fork or bottom of glass). Cookies will be very soft until they cool down.
5. Store these cookies in Ziploc bags or other airtight containers in refrigerator. Do not keep them in cookie jar, as they will stick together at room temperature and ants will have a feast.

********************************* IMPORTANT *********************************

These cookie recipes call for whole wheat pastry flour. This is NOT interchangeable with regular whole wheat flour. Made from softer wheat, pastry flour yields a more delicate texture and flavor to cookies, cakes, and pastries. If you absolutely cannot find whole wheat pastry flour, unbleached white flour will produce similar results, although nutritional value will be compromised. Please use whole wheat pastry flour, or the results will be disappointing.

Gingersnaps (virtually fat-free)

Makes 3-4 dozen cookies

Preparation time: 20 minutes plus overnight refrigeration, 15 minutes to form   Baking time: 10 minutes

Intensely flavored and satisfying, these chewy, spicy morsels will make your taste buds sing. The dough MUST be refrigerated overnight or longer for flavors to meld. A melon-baller will make the job easier and produce a more uniform shape.

2	c. minus 2 Tbsp. whole wheat pastry flour		1	tsp. cinnamon
¾	c. Sucanat® or brown sugar, firmly packed		1	Tbsp. ground ginger (or more for intense flavor)
2	tsp. baking soda			
2	Tbsp. cool water		½	c. prune purée
½	tsp. salt		¼	c. blackstrap molasses
½	tsp. ground cloves (or more for intense flavor)		2	tsp. Ener-G® egg replacer
			1	c. turbinado sugar, to coat (optional)

1. In medium mixing bowl, thoroughly mix flour, sugar, baking soda, salt, cloves, cinnamon, and ginger.
2. In separate bowl, thoroughly mix together prune purée and molasses.
3. In small glass, combine Ener-G® egg replacer with cool water. Mix well with fork. Add to prune mixture and stir. (Optional: Use 1 whole egg or 2 egg whites instead of Ener-G® egg replacer and water.)
4. Dump wet mixture into dry mixture. Using electric mixer, mix thoroughly. Or you may put on disposable kitchen gloves and mix it all up with your hands. Dough may be very crumbly and dry-looking at first; continue mixing until dough becomes sticky enough to form ball. DO NOT ADD MORE LIQUID!
5. Knead dough into smooth ball and wrap tightly in plastic cling wrap. Refrigerate overnight or longer. Do not skip this step!
6. After refrigerating overnight or longer, preheat oven to 350 degrees.
7. Unwrap chilled dough. Use melon-baller (lightly oiled, if needed) or rounded 1 tsp. measuring spoon to form dough into cherry-size balls.
8. Put turbinado sugar or white sugar in a shallow bowl. Roll cookie balls in sugar. (This step is optional, but more authentic and yields a more attractive cookie.) Place cookie balls on parchment-lined cookie sheet and press tops of cookies with bottom of glass to flatten. (Cookies expand a lot during baking.)
9. Bake 10 minutes. Do not overbake! Enjoy warm or cold. Wait about 5 minutes after taking the sheet out of the oven before removing cookies from parchment, but remove them while cookies are still slightly warm to avoid sticking.

About Prune Purée

Prune purée is frequently used in place of eggs and butter in cookie recipes. It yields a rich, moist cookie and is high in fiber and nutrients. If you don't want to make your own, use a commercially-prepared product such as Sunsweet Lighter Baker, Wonderslim, or even baby food prunes (in cake-type recipes). However, prune purée is a snap to make, and it's good to keep on hand for baking. Tightly covered, prune purée keeps for several weeks in the refrigerator.

2½ c. pitted prunes
⅔ c. very hot water

applesauce to taste

1. Toss prunes into blender. Add water. Blend on high speed until smooth, stopping occasionally to scrape down side of blender. (This will take a few minutes.)

2. Blend a little applesauce into the mixture if you wish. The end result should be thick and sticky, almost the consistency of stiff cookie dough.

Molasses-Raisin Cookies (fat-free)

Makes 40-50 cookies

Preparation time: 5 minutes plus cooling time

Baking time: 10 minutes

Loaded with iron and simple to make, these taste nuggets are sweetened only with molasses and raisins. The secret is in the method.

1   c. raisins
1⅓ c. water
¾   c. blackstrap molasses

3½ c. whole wheat pastry flour
1   tsp. baking soda
2   tsp. cinnamon

1. In small saucepan, combine water and raisins. Bring to boil. Remove from heat and add molasses. Let cool at least 10 minutes. Preheat oven to 350 degrees.
2. In mixing bowl, stir together flour, baking soda, and cinnamon.
3. Add cooled liquids to dry ingredients and mix thoroughly.
4. Drop dough onto parchment-lined cookie sheet using 2 spoons—1 to scoop and 1 to scrape dough onto cookie sheet.
5. Bake 10 minutes. Do not overcook!

It takes 4-5 pounds of fresh grapes to produce 1 pound of raisins.

Kashi® Candy (no-bake)

Makes 36-40 candies

Preparation time: 10 minutes

Believe it or not, this candy is actually good for you! Packed with raw, unsalted, shelled pumpkin seeds (pepitas), dried fruit, and Kashi® (puffed whole grain cereal), it is a good source of vitamin E, protein, and fiber. Brown rice syrup provides the "glue" that holds the candy together and adds a hint of sweetness. Use all-natural cranberries, such as Craisins by Ocean Spray, or Mariani brand.

2	c. raw, shelled, unsalted pumpkin seeds (pepitas)	½	c. raisins	
		½	c. dried cranberries	
2	c. plain Kashi® (puffed whole grain cereal)	⅔	c. brown rice syrup	

1. In a large nonstick frying pan, over medium heat, toast pumpkin seeds (pepitas) about 2 minutes or until they begin to make popping sounds. Stir frequently. Do not burn!
2. Add Kashi® (puffed whole grain cereal) and continue stirring until mixture smells toasty, about 2 minutes.
3. Add raisins and dried cranberries. Stir to combine.
4. Place 3 dozen mini-size paper baking cups in mini-muffin baking pans. Or use foil mini-size baking cups, which can stand on their own.
5. Drizzle brown rice syrup over everything. Stir immediately and continuously until everything is sticky. Lower heat but do not remove pan from heat. Mixture must remain hot while being scooped into paper baking cups to form candy balls.
6. Using 2 spoons, scoop at least 1 Tbsp. mixture (about the size of a walnut) into each baking cup. Work quickly so candy does not cool and harden too soon. Try to avoid touching mixture with your fingers, as it is very hot and sticky.
7. Refrigerate until cool. This will only take a few minutes. Store in refrigerator to retain crunchiness and keep ants away!

VARIATIONS: If you can't find Kashi®, use any type of puffed cereal. For larger candies, scoop into cupcake-size paper baking cups. If there is any remaining candy mixture, spread it out evenly on baking parchment and let cool. Break off pieces (like peanut brittle) and enjoy!

CLEANUP HINT

Fill frying pan with at least 1 inch water. Bring to boil. The boiling water will melt away the glue-like brown rice syrup and the pan will come clean immediately. NEVER scour or scrub the pan—it won't work and you'll just get frustrated. Let the hot water do all the work (no detergent needed).

Bean Cookies (fat-free)

Makes 3 dozen

Preparation time: 20 minutes

Baking time: 10 minutes

Exceptionally high in protein and fiber, these cookies are virtually fat-free. The beans replace the usual eggs and butter, giving a rich flavor and soft, chewy texture without the fat or cholesterol. Unlike most other cookie doughs, this dough cannot be made ahead and refrigerated, as it will dry out and turn rock-solid. Form cookies immediately after mixing dough, then bake promptly.

4	c. rolled oats	¾	c. date pieces (or chopped dates)
1	tsp. baking powder	1	c. navy beans (canned, with liquid)
1	tsp. baking soda	1	c. Sucanat® or brown sugar, firmly packed
1	tsp. cinnamon	1	tsp. vanilla extract

1. Measure rolled oats into blender. Cover tightly and process until very fine like flour. Do not remove lid while blender is operating!
2. Add baking powder, baking soda, and cinnamon to blender and process again for about 5 seconds. Pour all mixed dry ingredients into mixing bowl. Add dates. Stir.
3. In same blender combine beans, Sucanat®, and vanilla and process until creamy.
4. Pour blended bean mixture into mixing bowl with dry ingredients. Mix well with electric mixer. If dough seems dry, add 2 or 3 Tbsp. soymilk or water. You may need to stop the mixer, scrape dough off beater, and start again. Continue until all dry ingredients are incorporated into bean mixture and dough is stiff. Be patient!
5. Preheat oven to 350 degrees. Line cookie sheet with baking parchment. Drop dough by spoonful—1 spoon to scoop, the other to scrape dough off spoon onto parchment-lined cookie sheet. Form cookies about the size of a walnut. Press each cookie with bottom of glass to flatten slightly.
6. Bake for 10 minutes. Do NOT overbake! Remove from oven and enjoy warm or cool.

VARIATIONS: Great Northern, cannellini, or pinto beans may be substituted for navy beans. Other dried fruits such as raisins or apricots may be added. Date pieces, available in bulk at many health food stores, look like tiny cylinders and are dusted with oat flour.

Almond Thumbprint Cookies

Makes 3 dozen

Preparation time: 30 minutes

Baking time: 12-14 minutes

Delicious, nutritious, and attractive, these cookies contain no refined sugar and are very high in protein, calcium, fiber, and fat grams—but it's the "good" fat, from almonds. Get the kids to help with their thumbprints, and don't be afraid to experiment with different flavors of preserves.

1	c. raw almonds (to make 1½ c. almond meal)	⅔	c. frozen apple juice concentrate
1	c. whole wheat pastry flour	⅓	c. expeller-pressed canola oil
2	tsp. baking powder	1	tsp. almond extract
¼	tsp. salt	1	tsp. vanilla extract
		⅓	c. apricot jam

1. In blender, grind almonds into fine meal. You may need to stop blender and scrape down sides a couple of times. Keep lid on tightly when blender is operating, or almond "dust" will fly everywhere!
2. In medium bowl, mix together almond meal, flour, baking powder, and salt.
3. In blender, mix together apple juice concentrate, canola oil, and extracts.
4. Pour wet ingredients from blender into bowl with dry ingredients. Mix thoroughly with electric mixer. (Dough will be very stiff.) Preheat oven to 350 degrees.
5. Using 2 spoons—1 to scoop dough and 1 to scrape onto parchment-lined baking sheet.
6. Indent each cookie with thumb or finger. Drop about ½ tsp. fruit-sweetened apricot jam in each imprint.
7. Bake 10 to 12 minutes. Do NOT overbake! Remove cookies from oven and let sit for several minutes before removing from baking sheet. Cookies are very soft and cannot be handled without breaking until they cool down a bit. These cookies actually taste better the next day.

Pecan Cookies

Makes 3 dozen

Preparation time: 20 minutes

Baking time: 20-30 minutes

Very similar to Almond Thumbprint Cookies, these cookies are also very high in protein, fiber, and fat.

1¼	c. pecans	pecan halves for garnish
	Almond Thumbprint Cookie recipe	

Grind pecans in blender. This yields about 1½ c. finely ground pecan meal. Follow recipe for Almond Thumbprint Cookies, replacing almond meal with pecan meal. Instead of apricot jam, press half a pecan into top of each cookie.

Sugar-free Sugarplums (no-bake)   Makes 2-3 dozen

Preparation time: 15-20 minutes

These aren't really plums, and they do not contain sugar. We just didn't know what else to call them. Not quite candy, and definitely not cookies, these tantalizing treats defy description. Flavors are intense yet complex, and variations are endless. The dough is impossibly sticky, so use a melon-baller to form individual sugarplums instead of forming them with your hands. Experiment with your favorite liqueur (use half honey and half liqueur) and roll balls in chopped nuts, chocolate sprinkles, or whatever you fancy.

½	c. slivered almonds	2	Tbsp. honey (or 1 Tbsp. honey plus
4	oz. pitted dates, figs, and/or prunes		1 Tbsp. liqueur)
	(about 1 c.)	1-2	tsp. orange zest, finely grated
2	Tbsp. unsweetened cocoa	½	tsp. almond extract or vanilla extract
½	tsp. cinnamon		

COATING SUGGESTIONS: almond slivers or slices, raw or toasted

shredded coconut

chocolate sprinkles or other decorations

1. Toast almonds in skillet over medium heat, about 2 minutes. When slightly golden and aromatic, remove from heat and let cool briefly.
2. In food processor, grind toasted almonds into coarse crumbs. Add date/fig/prune mixture. Blend until crumbly, stopping to scrape down sides of blender, if necessary.
3. Add honey. Pulse until well combined, stopping to scrape down sides, as needed.
4. Using lightly oiled melon-baller or 1 tsp. measuring spoon, form mixture into walnut-size balls. Fill shallow bowls with your choice of coatings (see below). Roll sugarplum balls in coating.
5. Place on baking parchment or in mini-size baking cups (paper or foil). Cover tightly until ready to serve. Refrigeration is recommended because ants love this treat. These keep for several weeks—but they won't stay around that long!

Rice Pudding

Serves 8

Preparation and cooking time: 30 minutes, if rice is already cooked

A great way to use up leftover short-grain brown rice, this creamy comfort food has a hint of orange. So delicious and nutritious, it can be enjoyed the next morning for breakfast.

1	qt. soymilk or Almond Milk (plain or vanilla)	¼	tsp. salt
½	c. raisins	1	tsp. cinnamon
3	c. cooked short-grain brown rice	3	strips orange zest (2-3 inches each)
⅓	c. Sucanat®, honey, agave nectar, or brown sugar	2	tsp. vanilla extract

1. Combine all ingredients except vanilla extract in medium pot. Bring to boil, stirring occasionally. When mixture starts to thicken, reduce heat to simmer.
2. Continue stirring occasionally until mixture gets creamy. If a creamier texture is desired, stir in a little more soymilk. When desired consistency is reached, remove pudding from heat and stir in vanilla extract. (Pudding will continue to thicken a bit as it cools.)
3. Before serving, remove all orange zest from pudding. Orange flavor intensifies the longer the zest remains in the pudding, so don't leave it in for too long unless you love this flavor. Serve warm or chilled.

VARIATIONS: Experiment with other dried fruits such as apricots or dates. Use coconut or maple flavorings instead of vanilla. If you prefer, short grain white rice may be substituted for brown rice.

Tapioca Pudding

Serves 4

Preparation time: 1 minute   Resting time: 20 minutes   Cooking time: 15 minutes

Tapioca pudding is simple to make and even simpler to ruin. A small amount of tapioca goes a long way to thicken a lot of liquid. Sucanat® (evaporated natural sugar cane crystals) adds depth and character to an otherwise bland dessert. Do not substitute white sugar because flavor will be compromised.

1	qt. (4 c.) plus 1 c. soymilk or Almond Milk	1	tsp. vanilla extract
⅔	c. tapioca beads (the tiny ones)		cinnamon (dash)
½	c. Sucanat® or agave nectar		

1. In large nonstick pot, combine 4 c. soymilk or Almond Milk, tapioca beads, and Sucanat® or agave nectar. Stir and let rest for at least 20 minutes.
2. Turn on heat and bring mixture to gentle boil, stirring often to prevent scorching. Reduce heat and simmer on very low for another 10 minutes, or until tapioca beads are soft and translucent. Mixture will start to thicken and will thicken considerably when cooled. Stir in vanilla extract.

3. When pudding has cooled to lukewarm, add up to 1 cup soymilk or Almond Milk. Stir well. Pour or scoop pudding into serving bowls or stemware. Dust tops lightly with cinnamon, if desired. Refrigerate until serving.

Almond Tapioca

Serves 4

Preparation time: 1 minute   Resting time: 20 minutes   Cooking time: 15 minutes

Follow recipe for Tapioca Pudding, using Almond Milk (store-bought or homemade with blanched almonds—see Beverages and Frozen Treats) instead of soymilk. Use 2 tsp. almond extract instead of vanilla. Serve in individual bowls or stemware, topped with a few slivered almonds, if desired.

Coconut Tapioca (lower-fat)

Serves 4

Preparation time: 1 minute   Resting time: 20 minutes   Cooking time: 15 minutes

This recipe does not use coconut milk. However, a similar flavor can be achieved with almond milk and coconut extract. Simply follow the recipe for Almond Tapioca. Instead of vanilla extract, substitute 2 tsp. coconut extract. Use ⅔ c. agave nectar or mild light-colored honey instead of Sucanat®. Serve in individual bowls or stemware, topped with fruit, if desired. Peaches, nectarines, apricots, strawberries, raspberries, or blackberries are good choices.

Almond-Date Pie Crust (no-bake)

Makes 1 crust

Preparation time: 5 minutes plus soak time for nuts

This easy crust is ideal for any pie, tart, or cheesecake. High in protein, calcium, fiber and flavor, you won't believe how deliciously simple it is!

2   c. raw almonds
4-5   dates, pitted and chopped (about ¼ c.)
1   Tbsp. shredded raw coconut (optional)

1. Put almonds in deep bowl. Run very hot tap water over almonds. Let sit until water cools to lukewarm. Swish almonds, drain, and rinse well. (The soak water will turn brownish-red.) Repeat until soak water is clear.
2. Drain and rinse almonds. In food processor, combine dates and soaked almonds. Process until mixture is crumbly but not doughy or smooth.
3. Sprinkle coconut into bottom of pie pan or spring-form pan. Pour almond-date mixture into pan and spread evenly with moistened fingertips. Freeze for 10 minutes or until filling is ready.

Chocolate Tofu Cream Pie
(No-bake, nondairy)

Serves 8

Preparation time: 10 minutes or less

Chill time: 1 hour or more

This simple, decadent dessert is not the most healthful treat, but it is a delicious way to eat tofu and it is a good source of protein. Even a child can make it.

1 pkg. (10 oz.) good-quality dark chocolate chips
   (I recommend Ghirardelli)
1½ boxes (15-18 oz. total) silken Lite tofu (firm or
   extra firm)
1 tsp. almond extract or vanilla extract
¼ tsp. cinnamon
1 pie crust (Almond-Date Crust or store-bought graham
   cracker crust)

> *Chocolate comes from the cacao bean, which grows on cacao trees. It takes four hundred cacao beans to produce one pound of chocolate.*

1. Spread chocolate chips on glass plate. Microwave briefly until chips are soft but not completely melted— less than 2 minutes. Be careful not to burn them!
2. Meanwhile, crumble tofu into blender. Add almond or vanilla extract and softened chocolate chips. Blend until very smooth and creamy, scraping down sides of blender, as needed.
3. Pour contents of blender into graham cracker crust or Almond-Date Crust. Refrigerate uncovered for at least 1 hour, until very firm. Serve chilled.

Tipsy Chocolate Tofu Cream Pie

Serves 8

Preparation time: 10 minutes or less

Chill time: 1 hour or more

Follow previous recipe for Chocolate Tofu Cream Pie. Instead of almond extract and cinnamon, add 1 to 2 Tbsp. Amaretto, Kahlua, or Peppermint Schnapps. Blend very well, until silky smooth. Pour mixture into crust and chill at least 1 hour before slicing.

Chocolate Banana Cream Pie

Serves 8

Preparation time: 10 minutes

Chill time: 1 hour or more

Follow recipe for Chocolate Tofu Cream Pie. Slice or dice 2 perfectly ripe bananas and fold into the filling before pouring filling into crust. Chill at least 1 hour before slicing.

Peanut Butter Chocolate Cream Pie

Serves 8

Preparation time: 10 minutes

Chill time: 1 hour or more

Follow recipe for Chocolate Tofu Cream Pie. Add ¼ to ½ c. good-quality natural peanut butter to blender mixture and process until very smooth. Pour into pre-made crust and chill at least 1 hour before serving. You may adjust amount and type of peanut butter to suit your personal taste.

Pumpkin Un-Cheesecake

Serves 12-16

Preparation time: 20 minutes plus cooling time

Baking time: 1 hour

Made in a spring-form pan, this incredibly wonderful dessert is like an intense pumpkin cheesecake with a toasted pecan and date "crust." High in protein, fiber and beta-carotene, tofu replaces eggs, cream, and cheese so the filling is almost fat-free. This is the featured dessert at holiday dinners, and it's easy to make. Best if made a day or two ahead so flavors can meld.

CRUST:

1	c. pecans
1	c. date pieces (or use pitted dates), chopped
2	Tbsp. prune purée (see glossary)

FILLING:

1	box (12.3 oz.) silken tofu (firm or extra firm), crumbled	1	tsp. vanilla extract
1¾	c. canned pumpkin (do not use pumpkin pie mix)	1	tsp. cinnamon
		½	tsp. ground ginger
½	c. Sucanat® or brown sugar, densely packed	⅛	tsp. nutmeg
¼	c. pure maple syrup		ground cloves, pinch (optional)
2	Tbsp. molasses	2	tsp. arrowroot starch or cornstarch
		¼	c. soymilk or other non-dairy milk

1. Preheat oven to 350 degrees. Spread pecans on baking parchment. Place in oven and toast about 5 minutes, or until fragrant. Do not burn! When toasted, remove from oven and let cool.

2. Put dates and cooled toasted pecans in food processor. Pulse several times until pecans are chopped (but not too fine). Add prune purée and pulse again until mixed.

3. Cut a circle of baking parchment to fit bottom of spring-form pan. Pour date-pecan-prune mixture into pan and press evenly over bottom of pan. Bake for 5 minutes. Remove from oven.

4. Combine all filling ingredients in blender. Blend until absolutely creamy smooth, then blend some more.

5. Pour blended tofu mixture into prepared date-pecan "crust" and bake for 1 hour. Remove from oven and let cool completely before refrigerating. Chill overnight, uncovered. Top will slightly crack as it cools. Do not slice until well-chilled, as pie will "set" more.

6. Remove sides of spring-form pan and slice into at least 12 pieces. If desired, top each slice with dollop of Almond Cream (see Beverages & Frozen Treats).

VARIATION: Use rectangular glass baking pan. Slice dessert into small squares when chilled.

Gingerbread Cake

Preparation time: 15 minutes

Serves 16

Baking time: 35-45 minutes,
depends on type of pan

Fabulous, intensely flavored, and without added fat, this dark, delicious cake is rich in minerals. It can be made as a sheet cake, Bundt cake, or cupcakes. Prepare baking pan of choice. For a Bundt pan or 9x9-inch cake pan, lightly spray or coat with oil. For cupcakes, line muffin tins with paper baking cups.

¼	c. prune purée (see About Prune Purée)	½	tsp. salt
½	c. soymilk or other non-dairy milk	½	tsp. ground cloves (or more), to taste
¼	c. frozen orange juice concentrate (calcium-enriched)	2	tsp. ground ginger (or more), to taste
		2	tsp. cinnamon
2	Tbsp. flaxseed meal	1	tsp. orange zest, finely grated
¾	c. maple syrup	1	c. boiling water
½	c. blackstrap molasses	2	tsp. baking soda
½	c. Sucanat® or brown sugar	2	c. whole wheat pastry flour

1. Prepare baking pan of choice (see introduction to recipe). Preheat oven to 350 degrees.
2. Mix together all ingredients except water, baking soda, and flour and in large bowl, using wire whisk.
3. Add baking soda to boiling water and immediately pour into bowl with prune mixture. Stir well with whisk.
4. Gradually sprinkle flour and whisk into the mixture. Do not dump flour in all at once, because the hot mixture may cause the flour to become lumpy unless it is stirred in a little at a time.
5. When well combined, pour into prepared baking pan. Bake 35 to 45 minutes (about 20 minutes if making cupcakes), or until toothpick comes out clean when inserted into center of cake.

VARIATIONS: Add ½ to ¾ c. raisins to batter before adding hot water. Play with different amounts of spices, if you prefer it more or less spicy. A light glaze made with ¾ c. sifted powdered sugar and 1½ tsp. fresh lemon or lime juice (mix together in small bowl using fork) adds a surprising sweet-tart taste. Glazing is easier and neater if cake is glazed while frozen.

Maple-Ginger Fruit Crisp

Serves 6-8

Preparation time: 20 minutes

Baking time: 50 minutes

Bursting with seasonal fruits and enhanced with a touch of fresh ginger root and maple syrup, this simple dessert has endless possibilities. Try different fruits such as apples, pears, peaches, nectarines, strawberries, blueberries, raspberries, blackberries, mangos, and plums. Toss in a few cranberries if they are available. Combine two or three different fruits, fresh and/or frozen. If fresh fruit is not available or you are short on time, use frozen, unsweetened, whole berries, or canned peaches and pears. Topped with maple-sweetened toasted oats, this healthful dessert contains no refined sugar.

FILLING:

8	c. fruit, sliced (or whole berries, fresh or frozen)
1	Tbsp. fresh ginger root, peeled and grated (use more for added zing)
⅓	c. pure maple syrup
½	tsp. nutmeg
¼	c. lemon juice (juice from ½ lemon)
¾	c. maple syrup (do NOT substitute)
2	Tbsp. cornstarch or arrowroot starch

TOPPING:

2	c. rolled oats
2	tsp. cinnamon

1. Preheat oven to 350 degrees. In large bowl, mix together all filling ingredients.
2. Take 2 c. of this fruit mixture and put into blender with cornstarch or arrowroot starch. Blend until smooth. Pour puréed mixture back into bowl with fruit and stir to combine.
3. Lightly coat or spray inside (bottom and sides) of oblong baking dish (about 9x12x3 inches) with oil. Pour everything into baking dish. Make sure to allow at least 1½ inch head room. Put in oven.
4. Meanwhile, in small mixing bowl, combine and stir all topping ingredients.
5. Spread topping mixture evenly on parchment-lined baking sheet. Bake oats in oven on lower shelf for about 10 minutes at same time fruit mixture is baking.
6. Remove toasted topping from oven and cool briefly. When fruit mixture starts to bubble and thicken, (about 35 to 40 minutes) remove it from oven. (If fruit is frozen, this will take longer.) Scatter topping mixture evenly across top of fruit. Put fruit crisp back in oven and bake for another 5 to 10 minutes.
7. Remove from oven and let cool for at least 10 minutes. Serve warm, chilled, or at room temperature. Enjoy as dessert or even for breakfast!

VARIATIONS: Experiment with various fruits and combinations, using whatever is on hand. For extra zing, increase ginger root. NEVER substitute powdered ginger in this recipe.

THE ART OF READING AND UNDERSTANDING NUTRITION LABELS

Making the decision to change your way of eating and cooking is the beginning of a rewarding lifetime adventure. As you embark on this adventure, you may hit some rough spots in the road. Learning how to read labels is one of the first big (and ongoing) challenges. Nutrition labels are required by law on all packaged foods except those produced and sold only locally. They are intended to inform the consumer, but more often they confuse or mislead. Once you read and understand what the label really says, you'll never approach grocery shopping the same way. Just because something is sold at a health food store doesn't necessarily mean it's good for you. Here are some commonly misunderstood aspects of nutrition labels, and what to watch out for:

Serving size: Ask yourself, "Is the serving size realistic?" In the United States, if a serving contains less than .5 grams of fat it can claim to be fat-free. In Canada, however, if a product contains any amount of fat it cannot claim to be fat-free. So the identical "fat-free" product would not be fat-free in Canada, and it would require completely different labeling. Keep in mind that the serving size is often unrealistically small so that the manufacturer can claim it falls into the fat-free zone of less than half a gram (.5) per serving. The product may still be high in fat if you eat a normal size serving or several servings. Watch out!

Fat-Free, "Lite," 97% LESS FAT: Check the number of calories per serving. Then check the calories from fat. Divide the total calories per serving by the calories from fat to get the real percentage of fat per serving. Some products claim to be "Lite," yet the fat calories are abundant. Other "Lite" products have less fat but far more sugar, so the calorie content is still high and

the taste is also compromised. To be classified as Light or "Lite" the FDA requires the food to contain 30% fewer calories OR half the fat and half the sodium of the regular version of the same food, which doesn't mean it is actually a low-fat food. Certain olive oil blends claim to be "Lite," yet what the manufacturers really mean is that the oil tastes lighter because it is mixed with bland oils which reduce the distinctive taste of pure olive oil. The actual fat content is identical. Frequently, especially with processed deli meats, a label screams "97% less fat!" yet when you do the math, it doesn't compute. How can the company get away with this? They are calculating by weight, not by actual percentage of fat. Interestingly, certain margarines claim to be fat-free, yet when calculating the total calories divided by the number of fat calories, the percentage of fat calories is 100%. Obviously, the product is total fat, yet it claims to be fat-free.

Order of ingredients: Ingredients are listed from greatest to smallest amount. Therefore, the first ingredient is the primary ingredient in the product, and the last ingredient may be just a trace amount. A rule of thumb: If sugar or fat is in the first three ingredients listed, put the item back on the shelf. Often a manufacturer will attempt to disguise the true sugar content of an item by breaking the sugars into specific types of sugar by different names, to avoid having sugar appear as the first or second ingredient. Beware!

Other names for sugars/sweeteners: High fructose corn syrup, corn syrup solids, aspartame, honey, sugar, Splenda, brown sugar; these are just a few of the names for sweeteners. Did you know that most canned foods, including beans and other nutritious foods, have sugar added? Don't the manufacturers have enough confidence in the quality and flavor of their food to just let it be what it is and taste like itself without adding sugar? The same can be said about salt, in many cases. This is why most canned vegetables and legumes should be rinsed before eating.

Fats and Oils: Avoid anything that says hydrogenated or partially hydrogenated. The vast majority of fats and oils used in junk food, crackers, chips, cereals, and commercially prepared baked goods are made with hydrogenated fats and oils. Without getting into the chemistry of fats, just take my word for it. You DON'T want them in your diet, not even a little bit! By the way, even most chips found in health food stores are prepared with hydrogenated or partially hydrogenated oils. Avoid cottonseed oil in any form. Cottonseed oil comes from cotton, which is the most highly pesticide-contaminated crop in the world, and humans should not ingest pesticides. Palm oils and tropical oils should also be avoided because they are high in saturated fats.

Read labels carefully and avoid saturated fats if at all possible.

Cholesterol: Just because a food is labeled "cholesterol-free" doesn't mean it is fat-free or even lowfat. NO PLANT FOODS CONTAIN CHOLESTEROL. Even avocados, nuts, and olives—which are all high in fat—contain zero cholesterol. Palm oils (including coconut oil and so-called "tropical" oils) are high in saturated fats, yet they contain no cholesterol. So when you see your favorite brand of potato chips declaring itself cholesterol-free, remember that ALL potato chips are cholesterol-free because potatoes are plants and the oils they are fried in are plant-based. Yet the fat content is extremely high, and the serving sizes are generally small. Keep in mind that cholesterol-free advertising is a ploy to make the uneducated consumer choose that brand, even though every other brand of the same food is also cholesterol-free. All vegetables, fruits, nuts, grains, beans, and seeds are cholesterol-free, but farmers don't label their produce to advertise that fact.

Chemicals: If you can't pronounce it and you don't know what it is, then you probably shouldn't eat it. All sorts of chemicals are added to packaged foods, often as preservatives and flavor enhancers. Just because the FDA hasn't declared it harmful does not mean it is safe to eat.

The Bottom Line: Read, read, read!! Take your time shopping for food. Study the fine print. Eventually you will learn which companies produce packaged foods that are actually good for you, or at least not detrimental to your health. You may reach the same conclusion I did: It is better to prepare food from scratch, avoid canned or packaged goods (with only a few exceptions), and stick with fresh produce and wholesome bulk items. You'll save incredible amounts of money and improve your overall health and well-being by avoiding packaged, processed foods and focusing instead on fresh vegetables, fruits, nuts, legumes, and whole grains.

If you have to buy packaged or processed foods and you don't have time to do the math or read every detail on an ingredient list, remember these guidelines:

1. Avoid products with ingredients that include the words:
   Hydrogenated/partially hydrogenated
   Palm oils/tropical oils
   Unpronounceable multi-syllable words—usually chemical additives
2. Avoid products with oils or other fats and/or sweeteners in any form among the first three ingredients.

Dietary restrictions are merely detours on the road to culinary heaven. Rather than focusing on what we "shouldn't" or "can't" eat, let's begin a quest to discover new taste delights, starting with explorations of your local health food store, farmers' market, Asian market, and even the exotic foods section of your local supermarket. Think of adventure, not sacrifice. Think outside the box. You will be happily surprised at the amazing variety of delicious, healthful options available to you, no matter how restricted your diet may be.

COOKING TECHNIQUES AND TERMINOLOGY

Al denté: Cooking term used to describe cooked pasta that is almost tender yet firm. Literally, "to the tooth," pasta cooked al denté is perfectly cooked, not soggy or limp.

Baking: Cooking food in a preheated oven. Breads, pastries, cookies, desserts, pizza, and casseroles are baked. When vegetables and meats are baked (dry-cooked) in an oven, it is called roasting. The method is the same, but the terminology depends on the food.

Blanching: A parboiling technique; immersing ingredients in boiling water or other liquid and cooking for a very short time, no more than 30 seconds. For vegetables, blanching is used to intensify color and set flavor. Immediately after blanching, transfer vegetables to an icewater bath to stop the cooking process and set the color. For almonds, blanching is used to remove skins, and the end result is a smooth white nut. See How to Blanch Almonds in BEVERAGES AND FROZEN TREATS.

Blending: Combining ingredients and processing until very smooth, indistinguishable, and uniform in texture, usually in a blender. A high-performance blender can emulsify almost any ingredient, including nuts and ice.

Boiling: Cooking food by keeping it submerged in boiling water for an extended time. Not appropriate for vegetables, as it removes many nutrients, boiling is best used for cooking pasta and certain grains and beans. With boiling, be sure to have enough liquid. Boiling techniques vary according to the type of food being boiled. See separate sections on how to cook pasta, grains, and beans.

Caramelize: To cook over low heat until the sugars in the ingredient becomes slightly sweet. Caramelizing reduces the ingredient to its flavorful essence, adding extra depth and "warmth" to sauces, soups, and other dishes. Onions are typically caramelized. Butter and sugar are often cooked together until caramelized.

Chiffonade: To slice into very fine strips. Usually used with leafy herbs like basil. Stack leaves, roll, then slice across the center vein. Strips should be no more than ⅛-inch wide.

Chopping: Cutting food into uniform-sized pieces by using quick heavy downward strokes with a sharp knife or cleaver. Chopped food is more coarsely cut than minced food. White polyethylene cutting boards and flexible plastic cutting surfaces are recommended because they are easy to clean, can be washed in the dishwasher, are less likely to harbor bacteria, and they will not blunt your knives.

Combining: Putting ingredients together. In this book, any recipe that instructs you to combine also indicates exactly how to combine and what to do with the ingredients that you have just put together.

Dicing: Cutting food into tiny (⅛ to ¼-inch) pieces. To dice vegetables, cut vegetables in slices, stack the slices, cut them into strips, then cut the strips, lengthwise into small cubes. To dice tofu, cut a block of drained tofu into equal slices, then stack the slices and cut into strips. Cut these strips into cubes.

Draining: Removing water or moisture, usually using a colander or strainer. To drain pasta, put colander in sink and dump cooked pasta into colander. Allow to drain before combining pasta with other ingredients. To drain tofu, wrap a block of firm or extra-firm tofu in a cotton tea-towel. First fold towel in half, lengthwise, then place tofu on one end of towel and roll tightly in towel. Let sit until towel is completely saturated. Repeat with fresh towel for a dryer, firmer tofu. See section on Tofu Basics in SAUCES, SPREADS, AND SNACKS for more information.

Folding: A technique for adding air to batter while incorporating a heavier ingredient into a lighter one. Use a rubber spatula to cut repeatedly through the batter in a down, across, and upward motion.

Forking: Extracting the juice from citrus fruits, especially lemons and limes, using a fork. See How to Fork a Lemon in SALADS AND DRESSINGS.

Freezing: Preserving by subjecting to very cold temperature. Most grains, beans, fruits, vegetables, and soups can be successfully frozen. Freezing causes liquids and soft foods to harden. Juices and smoothies can be poured into molds and frozen to make Popsicles. Freeze soups and beans in glass jar with tightly sealed lid, allowing plenty of head room because liquids expand a lot as they freeze. Most fruits and vegetables can be successfully frozen in ziplock-style plastic freezer bags. Frozen tofu that has been thawed and drained takes on a chewy, meat-like texture. To freeze tofu, follow instructions under Tofu Basics in SAUCES, SPREADS, AND SNACKS. Never freeze potatoes or anything with potatoes as an ingredient.

Grating: Shredding or pulverizing by rubbing food against a grater. Carrots and the zest of citrus fruits are commonly grated.

Grinding: Crushing into fine particles, usually using a blender, coffee grinder, or mortar and pestle. Grinding breaks down the hard outer shell and creates a more

digestible food. Grinding also releases the flavors of spices. Flaxseed is ground into flaxseed meal using a high-performance blender. Nuts, seeds, and certain whole grains may be ground in a blender or coffee grinder. Spices are ground with a mortar and pestle.

Half-moons: Cutting technique used for elongated vegetables like carrots, Japanese eggplant, and zucchini. Cut vegetable in half, lengthwise (horizontally), then cut each piece across into half-circle pieces.

Julienne: To cut into uniform long thin slices, usually ⅛ to ¼-inch in width. Julienned vegetables look like matchsticks, more or less.

Marinating: Soaking in flavorful liquid before cooking. For maximum absorption of liquid, warm marinade is better absorbed by chilled foods, and cold marinade is best absorbed by warm foods. Tofu should be very well drained and "squeezed" (by wrapping in a towel) before marinating, or liquid will not be absorbed. Squeezing the tofu almost dry allows it to absorb marinade, just like squeezing a sponge dry allows it absorb more moisture.

Mashing: Breaking down vegetables, beans, or tofu with a handheld potato masher or fork. Press forcefully down on the food, repeating until desired consistency is achieved. An electric mixer or food processor may also be used for mashing large amounts of food. When mashing vegetables or tofu, add salt and other seasonings while mashing to ensure even seasoning.

Matchsticks: To make matchsticks, first cut the fruits or vegetables into thin, diagonal slices. Then stack these slices and cut into long, thin pieces about the size of matchsticks.

Mincing: Dicing foods very finely, not necessarily in uniform bits. Fresh herbs, garlic, and ginger are commonly minced.

Mixing: Combining or blending so that the ingredients are indistinguishable. Different utensils or appliances can be used, depending on the type of food to be mixed.

Peeling: Removing the outermost covering of a fruit, vegetable, or egg. A vegetable peeler or small sharp knife is most often used to peel fruits and vegetables. See note on How to Pit Olives and Peel Garlic in THE MAIN EVENT.

Pitting: Removing the pit from a food such as cherries, prunes, peaches, nectarines, dates, and olives. See note on How to Pit Olives and Peel Garlic in THE MAIN EVENT.

Preheating: Preheat oven about 10 minutes before using it, to ensure even heat distribution while baking or roasting food. Make sure oven has reached desired temperature before putting food in the oven. An oven thermometer is an excellent investment, as most ovens are not precise in their temperature readings.

Pressure cooking: Method of cooking which uses the force of intense steam pressure to cook food rapidly and evenly. Pressure cooking is done in a special pot called a pressure cooker.

Puréeing: To turn food into thick creamy "sauce" by processing in a blender, food processor, food mill, or by forcing it through a strainer. See About Prune Purée in SWEET ENDINGS.

Roasting: Cooking vegetables and meats over a high, dry heat. Usually done in an oven, over a flame, or a hot dry skillet (for seeds and spices). Roasting seals in the natural juices and flavors of food.

Sautéing: Quickly cooking foods in a very small amount of oil or other liquid over high heat on the stovetop. Lightly "frying." Similar to stir-frying.

Seeding: Removing seeds from vegetables and fruits, especially bell peppers, chile peppers, and cucumbers. Removing seeds from chile peppers greatly reduces their "heat." Wear gloves when seeding hot chile peppers!

Shredding: Cutting or tearing into long, thin, irregular strips, usually with a knife or food processor.

Simmering: Cooking food submerged in liquid over very low heat, not boiling. Many recipes call for bringing the food to boiling, then reducing heat and simmering for a specified length of time.

Slicing: Cutting into thin, broad pieces. Slice most vegetables on the diagonal (about 45 degrees). Slice tofu vertically into "cutlets" about ½-inch each. To slice an onion into "moons," cut in half from root to stem and place the flat half on a cutting board. Slice along growth lines into ¼-inch moons.

Soaking: Reconstituting sun-dried tomatoes or dried mushrooms by covering with very hot or boiling water. Let soak for 10 to 20 minutes, or until fairly soft. Drain and save soaking liquid for soups, sauces, and spreads such as hummus.

Steaming: Cooking vegetables by suspending them above (but never actually touching) boiling water. Use a steamer (collapsible metal steamers are convenient and inexpensive) and try seasoning the water below the steamer with vegetable broth or Bragg Liquid Aminos. Steaming retains flavor and nutrients of the vegetables.

Stir-frying: Quickly frying vegetables and other small bits of food at high heat in a very small amount of hot oil or liquid, stirring throughout the entire process to ensure even, fast cooking. Ingredients must be somewhat uniform in size (julienne cut preferred) so they will cook quickly and evenly. Cook each food in order of its cooking time, starting with the heaviest and driest (e.g. carrots) and ending with the most delicate (e.g. tomatoes, sprouts). Cook only until vegetables are crisp-tender but still brightly colored. A wok is perfect for stir-frying and uses less oil, but a large nonstick frying pan can be used if you don't have a wok.

INGREDIENTS AND UTENSILS

Learning about unfamiliar foods, what they look like, where to buy them, how to cook them, what they taste like, etc., can be challenging. Don't be afraid to try new things, your taste buds and your whole body will thank you. This glossary offers an introduction to some less familiar ingredients and cooking utensils.

Agave nectar: A natural, mild sweetener made from the juice of the agave plant, a succulent that grows in Mexico, South America, and the Southwestern United States. Agave nectar has a much lower glycemic index than honey, maple syrup, or sugar. It does not crystallize and dissolves instantly even in cold liquids.

Alaea Sea Salt: a type of coarse salt popular in Hawai'i, made from sea salt mixed with red Hawaiian clay. It is orange-red in color and contains a variety of trace minerals.

Almond milk: A milk-like beverage made from almonds in a blender. Make it yourself (easy!) or buy it in a health food store.

Arrowroot: A finely powdered starch used as a thickening agent instead of cornstarch. It does not alter the taste of foods prepared with it. A small amount of arrowroot will thicken a lot of liquid. Arrowroot becomes translucent and takes on a beautiful sheen when cooked. Excellent for sauces, gravies, and desserts.

Arame: Slightly sweet, delicately flavored sea vegetable. Arame come in thin strands and are available in Asian markets.

Arugula: Also called roquette or rocket. A delicate leafy lettuce with a distinct peppery bite. Fragile, pricey and sold by the ounce, it is best to buy arugula very fresh and use it within 24 hours. Try growing your own—it grows like a weed!

Bamboo mat: A small rectangular mat made of bamboo, used for making sushi.

Balsamic vinegar: Aromatic, slightly sweet, somewhat syrupy, and worth every penny, balsamic vinegar is used in dressings and seasonings, and as a condiment. A little goes a long way. Do NOT substitute!

Barley malt sweetener: A very mild sweetener with a dark, malty flavor. Made from sprouted, dried barley, it is about half as sweet as refined sugars and is more evenly metabolized. Found in health food stores.

Bean thread: Sometimes called cellophane noodles, bean thread is a type of very thin, translucent, threadlike noodle made from mung beans.

Better than Milk: A brand of powdered "milk" made from tofu. Dairy-free, it dissolves easily and tastes very, very good. Available in plain and vanilla and found in most health food stores.

Blackstrap molasses: Molasses that comes from the bottom of the barrel during processing of sugar cane into sugar. Blackstrap molasses is extremely rich in iron, calcium, potassium, phosphorus, and other minerals from the leaves of the sugar cane plant. Use just like regular molasses, but be prepared for a more intense flavor.

Bok choy: Chinese vegetable with green leaves on flat white stalks. Slightly sweet, crisp, and mild, bok choy is popular in stir-fries and as a side dish. Sometimes called Chinese cabbage.

Bragg Liquid Aminos: An unfermented all-purpose liquid seasoning made from vegetable protein. Similar to soy sauce (shoyu), but without added salt. Used as a condiment and flavoring for soups, salads, dressings, casseroles, stir-fries, etc. Bragg Liquid Aminos can also be mixed with water to make a quick broth for soups and gravies. Do NOT substitute with soy sauce. Available in health food stores.

Brown rice syrup: A very mild sweetener made from brown rice, it is more gradually metabolized than refined sugar. Found in health food stores. Lundberg's brand is preferred.

Buckwheat: A plant with small nutritious seeds. Buckwheat is not a type of wheat or grain, but a member of the rhubarb family. Buckwheat is gluten-free and can be purchased as flour, groats, or kasha.

Bulgur: Wheat that has been precooked, dried, and cracked, available in various textures from coarse to fine. Light and nutty-tasting, bulgur is the basis for tabouli and other Middle Eastern dishes. To prepare, cover bulgur with boiling water and let sit for 20 minutes or until water is absorbed, then proceed with recipe.

Capers: The pickled buds of a Mediterranean flowering plant, capers come in various sizes. Their flavor is vinegary and olive-like. Look for them next to the olives in any supermarket.

Chèvre: A type of goat cheese similar to cream cheese.

Chickpeas: Also known as garbanzo beans, chickpeas are widely used in Middle Eastern cooking. They look a lot like shelled hazelnuts.

Cilantro: Also known as Chinese parsley or fresh coriander, this flat-leaf herb has a uniquely pungent flavor. Commonly used in Mexican and Indian dishes, cilantro's distinctive flavor is impossible to ignore. You either love it or hate it. To store cilantro, stand it in a glass of water, cover it with a plastic bag and refrigerate the whole thing.

Congee: A soupy Chinese porridge made from rice or other grains. Eaten with vegetables and condiments.

Couscous: Tiny bits of precooked, dried wheat pasta common in North African and Middle Eastern dishes. Quick to prepare, it requires only 5 to 10 minutes of soaking, depending on the temperature of the water and desired texture of the couscous.

Daikon: Long white Japanese radish, eaten cooked, raw, or pickled.

Dates/Date pieces: The edible fruit of a tropical palm, dates add a moist, chewy sweetness and plenty of fiber to many recipes. For cooking, use date pieces purchased in bulk at a health food store. They look like tiny cylinders dusted with oat flour. This will save the cook a lot of time and effort, since these date pieces require no pitting or chopping.

Dulse: A slightly salty, nutty-tasting, reddish purple sea vegetable, rich in potassium, iron and magnesium.

Edamame: Soybeans in the pod, found in bags in the frozen food section of any supermarket. A delicious, high-protein, fun snack.

Ener-G® egg replacer: A powdered, egg-free product that, when mixed with water and stirred, can be use instead of eggs in many baked goods. Made with starches, it is cholesterol-free and fat-free. It contains no preservatives, sodium or sugar. Sold in a box under the brand name Ener-G® and available in health food stores.

Extracts: Flavorings used in desserts, extracts come in a multitude of flavors. Best to use "real" extracts instead of artificial, if available. The price difference may be substantial, but the results are worth it and a little of the real thing goes a very long way. Most commonly used extracts in this cookbook are vanilla, almond, and coconut.

Extra virgin olive oil: Use only the real thing. Never use "Lite," as it simply means the flavor is bland but the number of calories and fat grams are the same. Extra virgin olive oil is cold-pressed and smokes at a relatively low temperature. A little goes a long way for sautéing and stir-frying. For pasta sauces and other dishes, add a light drizzle of olive oil just before serving (instead of during preparation). This maximizes the flavor without adding lots of extra calories. Extra virgin olive oil is the basis for most vinaigrettes and other salad dressings in this book.

Fennel: A plant with aromatic seeds and a bulbous celery-like stalk with feathery leaves. The seeds are used as a spice. Fresh fennel has a licorice-like flavor.

Flaxseed/Flaxseed meal: A small, hard, shiny brown or golden seed rich in Omega-3 fatty acids. Flaxseeds must be ground into meal (use a blender or coffee grinder) to break the hard outer surface so they can be digested. Sprinkle flaxseed meal on cereal or other

dishes. Flaxseeds and flaxseed meal soaked in water become a gooey gel and can be used as a binder instead of egg whites. Flaxseeds and flaxseed meal are sold in health food stores. Look for Bob's Red Mill brand. Store flaxseed meal tightly sealed in the freezer or refrigerator, as flaxseeds are highly perishable once they are ground into meal, especially if overheated or exposed to air.

Flaxseed oil: The oil pressed from flaxseeds. Keep refrigerated. Never, ever use flaxseed oil in cooking. Used mainly in dressings and as a supplement, the health benefits make it worth the very high price. Available in the refrigerator section of health food stores. Buy only as much as you can use within a few weeks, as flaxseed oil oxidizes rapidly. Flaxseed oil can be kept frozen for up to a year, if you buy too much.

Garbanzo beans: Another name for chickpeas, this popular bean is widely used in Middle Eastern cooking.

Gomasio: A Japanese condiment made of sesame seeds and dried sea vegetables.

Gremolata: A garnish/condiment made of lemon zest, parsley, and garlic.

Hoisin sauce: A classic Chinese spicy-sweet sauce (fat-free), used as a dip or for cooking. Found in Asian markets and many supermarkets. Lee Kum Kee is an excellent brand.

Hummus: A traditional Middle Eastern spread made of chickpeas, tahini, garlic, and lemon.

Immersion blender: A slender hand-held wand blender designed to mix/blend soft foods and liquids. Versatile and convenient, use it to blend drinks right in the glass or purée soups and sauces right in the pot. Inexpensive (less than $20) and widely available.

Jicama: A large turnip-shaped root vegetable. Rough, brown, and ugly on the outside, the inside is crisp and almost sweet. High in potassium, jicama retains its crunch even when cooked. Flavor and texture is similar to water chestnuts.

Kabocha: Squat green or green and white winter squash (pumpkin) with dense, flavorful orange flesh. Also called Hokkaido pumpkin.

Kalamata olives: Intensely flavored almond-shaped black or dark purple olives from Greece. Essential in many dishes, NEVER substitute any other olives for Kalamata olives. Found in Middle Eastern delis and some supermarkets.

Kamut: An ancient grain related to wheat, used in place of wheat in cooking and baking. Kamut can also be combined with other whole grains and cooked like rice or used in pilaf.

Kashi®: A brand of fat-free cereal made with various toasted, puffed whole grains, found in health food stores and most supermarkets.

Kombu (Kelp): A sea vegetable, sold in dried dark-green flat strips, kombu is a natural flavor enhancer and tenderizer. Rich in calcium and iodine, kombu is a nutritious and flavorful salt substitute.

Liquid smoke: Distilled from hickory wood smoke, a few drops of this intense liquid imparts a deep, smoky aroma and flavor of ham or bacon. Great in beans, soups, or marinades for tofu. My personal favorite is split pea soup with liquid smoke.

Mandoline: A utensil for thin, uniform slicing. My favorite is the ceramic slicer by Kyocera, a convenient, easy-to-clean device with a double-edged ceramic blade so it slices twice as fast (coming <u>and</u> going!) The ceramic blade retains its sharpness and will not alter the taste or color of foods.

Maple syrup: The boiled-down sap of the sugar maple, not to be confused with maple-flavored syrup. Used as a natural flavoring and sweetener in many recipes, real maple syrup is expensive and worth every penny. Blended with flaxseed oil, it makes a thick, "buttery" pancake syrup.

Melon-baller: A small hand-held device that looks like a tiny ice cream scoop, used for scooping out the flesh of melons and forming into small balls about 1-inch in diameter. Also good for shaping cookies and other confections into uniform spheres.

Mesclun: Mixed greens used in salads, including flavorful, spicy varieties of lettuces and other greens.

Microplane: A hand-held rasp for finely grating ginger, citrus zest, hard cheese, etc.

Muesli: A Swiss-inspired breakfast cereal made with rolled oats, whole grains, flakes, nuts, seeds, and dried fruits. Serve with soymilk or other milk-type beverage, or topped with plain yogurt and fresh fruits.

Millet: A quick-cooking, nutty-flavored, tiny, round, golden grain from Africa. Millet becomes light and fluffy when cooked, and can be used like couscous or in pilafs. Cooked longer or in more liquid, millet becomes like mush. Millet is easy to digest and gluten-free. Uncooked millet looks exactly like uncooked quinoa, so label the grains when storing them. Available in health food stores.

Miso: A salty fermented paste made from cooked, aged soybeans and sometimes barley or rice. A highly nutritious, flavorful base for soups and sauces, miso should NEVER be boiled. A staple in Japanese cooking, miso comes in several colors and varieties. Lighter miso is more mellow and delicate than dark miso. Available in health food stores, Asian markets, and some supermarkets. Keep refrigerated.

Mung beans: Small green or yellow round beans. When dried, peeled, and split they are yellow and known as mung dahl (or moong dahl) in India. Bean sprouts are mung beans that have been soaked and sprouted.

Naan: A type of Indian flatbread, usually oblong or oval in shape.

Nayonaise: An eggless mayonnaise substitute made with organic soybeans. Found in health food stores.

Nori: Thin, crispy sheets of pressed, dried seaweed. Used as a wrapper for sushi or crumbled as a garnish, nori is rich in vitamin A and protein. Found in Asian markets and many supermarkets.

Nutritional yeast: Delicate yellow flakes or powder with a light cheese-like flavor and pleasant aroma, nutritional yeast is used as a flavoring or condiment and as "breading" for baked tofu. Red Star T6635+ brand is a reliable source of vitamin B_{12}. Nutritional yeast is NOT a leavening agent and cannot be substituted. It is sold by weight and seems pricey, but it is actually quite inexpensive because it weighs almost nothing and a little goes a long way. Nutritional yeast is (or should be) a staple in every vegan's kitchen. Available in health food stores, usually in the bulk section.

Orzo: A small, quick-cooking rice-shaped pasta common in Middle Eastern cooking. Available in health food stores and some supermarkets and ethnic grocery stores.

Parchment paper (baking parchment): A sturdy, heatproof, stick-resistant paper used to line baking pans and cookie sheets. Essential in fat-free baking, as nothing can stick or burn onto parchment. Use instead of foil. Available in many supermarkets and kitchen specialty shops. A little-known fact: baking parchment that has been used can be washed (by hand) and reused, as long as it has not been in contact with meat, dairy, or eggs. Simply wash with warm water and detergent, rinse very well, and place flat on oven rack to dry. (Do not turn on the oven.) Once you have discovered baking with parchment, you'll never again use foil to line a pan.

Pita: A middle Eastern flat, round bread. Some varieties can be opened and stuffed with fillings. Use as a dipping bread for hummus, or a crust for individual pizzas. Also called pocket bread.

Polenta: A thick cornmeal mush from northern Italy, or the type of coarse cornmeal from which the mush is made. Polenta "mush" can be baked, fried, grilled, or eaten, as is. Polenta-style cornmeal has more texture and character than regular cornmeal, and produces a heartier, more interesting cornbread.

Polyethylene cutting board: A cutting board made of polyethylene (a type of plastic), ideal for chopping and slicing anything. Polyethylene does not dull knife blades, and it does not retain odors, stains, or bacteria when properly washed. Best of all, it can be washed in the dishwasher!

Portabella: A very large, brown mushroom with an open flat cap. The caps can be grilled, broiled, or sautéed. They can be sliced or served whole. Portabellas (sometimes spelled Portobello) have a meaty texture and flavor. Remove the woody stem before cooking.

Pressure cooker: A special pot with a lid that seals tightly and has a steam release valve. By applying the force of intense steam, a pressure cooker can cook meats, vegetables, grains, and beans in a fraction of the normal time.

Prune purée: A "paste" made of prunes and water blended together until creamy. Use in baking (especially cookies) to replace eggs and butter, and to add flavor, fiber, and nutrients. Commercially prepared prune purée goes under the name of Wonderslim, Sunsweet Lighter Baker, or just plain baby food prunes. See About Prune Purée in SWEET ENDINGS.

Quinoa: An ancient grain of the Incas, quinoa contains more high-quality protein than any other grain. It has a mild, nutty taste and looks like millet. Before cooking, rinse well to remove a natural, bitter protective resin. When cooked, quinoa expands to five times its original size and each grain has a tiny spiral "tail." Use in salads, pilafs, casseroles, or even as porridge for breakfast. Low in gluten, quinoa is especially good for people with wheat sensitivity.

Rapadura: Evaporated sugar cane syrup. See Sucanat®.

Rice: Brown, white, black, purple, short-grain, long-grain, sweet, nutty; rice comes in numerous varieties and can be used for salads, dessert, casseroles, sushi, soup, pilaf, and countless other dishes. Rule of thumb: short-grain is softer, starchier, and a bit sweeter than long-grain. Use short-grain for rice pudding, paella, sushi, risotto, and soup. Long-grain works well in pilaf and salads. Combine several varieties of rice and cook according to time required for the longest cooking rice. Avoid using processed rice such as Minute Rice and Uncle Ben's. Lundberg's brand is highly recommended.

Rice cakes: Round disks made of puffed rice and sometimes various seasonings. Lundberg's has several excellent flavors of brown rice cakes, such a Sesame-Tamari and Wild Rice cakes. Lundberg's rice cakes make a great snack, especially with bean dips and other spreads in this cookbook. Avoid plain white rice cakes; they taste like Styrofoam.

Rice paper wrappers: Thin, translucent, fat-free wrappers made from rice flour. Used as wrapping for spring rolls and summer rolls.

Sesame oil: A staple in Asian cooking, use only the dark sesame oil made from toasted sesame seeds. Intensely flavorful, only a few drops (⅛ to ¼ tsp.) are needed to flavor an entire wok-full of stir-fried food. Found in the oils section of any supermarket or in Asian markets.

Soba: Long noodles made of buckwheat and other flours. From Japan, soba is used in salads and stir-fries.

Soymilk: Nondairy milky liquid made from soybeans, used as a substitute for milk. Flavor, nutrition, and fat content vary widely from brand to brand. Read label carefully to assess which is best for your needs. Do NOT use as infant formula.

Spring-form pan: A round, straight-sided pan for baking cakes and cheesecakes whose sides can be unclamped from the base for easy removal without disturbing the top.

Sriracha: Hot chili sauce popular in southeast Asian cuisine, containing chili, sugar, salt, garlic, and vinegar.

Steamer basket: Metal or bamboo "basket" with small holes, designed to hold foods in a pot above boiling water so that the food will cook by steam. Metal steamers usually collapse to fit various amounts of food and different sizes of pots.

Sucanat®: A brand name natural, unrefined sweetener made from evaporated sugar cane juice. Dark and richly flavored, it is often used in place of brown sugar. Also known as Rapidura. Available in health food stores.

Sun-dried tomatoes: Tomatoes that have been dried in the sun, producing a chewy texture and deep, rich, tart-sweet flavor. Sold in jars (usually packed in olive oil) or in their dried state in small cellophane bags, sun-dried tomatoes enhance the flavor of pasta, salads, and almost any dish. To reconstitute sun-dried tomatoes, pour boiling water over tomatoes in a mug. Wait awhile (around 10 minutes) to allow tomatoes to soften and expand. Do not throw away the soaking liquid. Use it for soups, broth, hummus, salad dressings, etc.

Tahini: Sesame butter, made from ground sesame seeds. An essential ingredient in Middle Eastern cooking, tahini is used in various dips, sauces, and spreads (such as hummus). Refrigerate after opening and stir well when it separates. Found in health food stores near the peanut butter and in Middle Eastern markets.

Tapioca: A starch obtained from the cassava root used to thicken desserts and sauces. The main ingredient in Tapioca Pudding.

Tea-towel: A small cotton or linen kitchen towel, not terry cloth.

Thai chili paste: A hot sauce originating in Thailand, including garlic, chilies, and sugar. Used to enliven various recipes. Available in Asian markets and some supermarkets.

Tofu: A highly versatile soy product made from soymilk and coagulated with nigari or calcium salt. An excellent source of minerals and complete protein, it is sold in rectangular containers. Bland on its own, it easily absorbs flavors and comes in various textures and consistencies. See Tofu Basics in SAUCES, SPREADS, AND SNACKS for more information.

Turmeric: A main ingredient in curry powder, a very small amount of turmeric (less than ¼ tsp.) can color an entire dish. Perfect for egg-style, tofu-based dishes and anything where a distinct golden-yellow color is desired (without changing the flavor). Add a pinch of turmeric while cooking food. Stir well to disperse. Yellow color intensifies as the temperature of the food increases, so start out with a very small amount of turmeric and increase, if necesary. Turmeric can stain, so be careful.

Vegenaise®: A delicious, creamy mayonnaise substitute that contains no animal or soy products. It comes in two versions. I prefer the kind made with grapeseed oil.

Vinegars: Available in a huge variety of flavors and colors, here are some of the vinegars you will want to keep on hand:

Apple cider vinegar: Made with apple cider, this light brown vinegar is great for salad dressings and is said to have healing properties.

189

Balsamic vinegar: A marvelous Italian vinegar with mellow, rich, subtly sweet undertones. Dark brown and opaque in color and very pricey, a little balsamic vinegar will greatly enhance salad dressings, sauces, and other dishes. Balsamic vinegar can also be used on its own as a dip for focaccia or other rustic varietal breads. If a recipe specifies balsamic vinegar, do NOT substitute with any other vinegar.

Raspberry vinegar: Slightly sweet, this vinegar is made with raspberries. Excellent in vinaigrettes or dressings for fruit salads.

Red wine vinegar: Good for vinaigrettes and other salad dressings and condiments; and as a marinade.

Rice vinegar: Low to moderate in acid, rice vinegar has a warm, mellow flavor and transparent color. Sprinkle on pasta salads and potato salads to add flavor and moisture without calories. Do not confuse this with the sweetened version of rice vinegar for sushi.

Distilled white vinegar: Keep this with your cleaning supplies. It's good for washing windows.

Vital wheat gluten: Protein formed when hard wheat flour is moistened and agitated. Vital wheat gluten is a wheat powder with all the carbohydrate and starch removed. Used in baking yeast breads to aid in leavening and to improve texture and elasticity. Vital wheat gluten is sometimes called gluten flour.

Vegetarian chili mix: A dried mixture of texture vegetable protein (TVP) made of soy, combined with piquant spices and bits of onion and herbs. Found in the bulk section of some health food stores, it is a great flavor- and texture-enhancer for chili, soups, and Mexican dishes.

Vegetarian stir-fry sauce: A shiitake mushroom-based bottled sauce used in place of oyster sauce in stir-fries and Asian cooking. Available in some Asian markets. Lee Kum Kee brand is excellent.

Whole wheat pastry flour: A type of very fine flour made from a softer wheat, used in baking cookies, cakes, quick-breads, pastries, and in place of white flour in cooking. Do not substitute with regular whole wheat flour. Do not use pastry flour for yeast breads, as the results may be disappointing due to low gluten content of whole wheat pastry flour.

Won bok: Also called Napa cabbage, this calcium-rich Chinese cabbage should not be cut or shredded until just before adding to the dish being prepared, to prevent calcium loss. A great addition to stir-fries, or use in place of regular cabbage.

Yogurt: A custard-like food prepared from milk curdled by bacteria. Common in Indian and Middle Eastern cooking, yogurt has a slightly tart flavor and aids in digestion. Be sure to use only plain, gelatin-free yogurt made of milk from cows that have not been treated with antibiotics and growth hormones.

Zest: The thin, colored outer layer of citrus fruits, used to flavor many desserts. Some recipes call for grated zest, others for strips of zest. Remove strips of zest from dish before serving.

RESOURCES

The following companies provide products that are specifically mentioned in this cookbook. If you have difficulty locating these products in your area, please contact the companies directly.

Barlean's Organic Oils

4936 Lake Terrell Road
Ferndale, WA 98248
1-800-445-3529
www.barleans.com

Known for their lignan-rich, good-tasting, 100% organic, pesticide-free flax oil, Barlean's was voted the world's leading brand of flax oil.

Better Than Milk

Division of Fuller Life, Inc.
1628 Robert C. Jackson Drive
Marysville, TN 37801
1-800-227-2320
www.betterthanmilk.com

A low-fat, lactose-free, cholesterol-free, caseinate-free, gluten-free, soy-based vegan beverage mix. A truly delicious, convenient, healthful, nondairy milk substitute, Better Than Milk can be used just like powdered milk.

Blendtec®

1206 South 1680 West
Orem, UT 84058
1-800-BLENDTEC (253-6383)
www.blendtec.com

Distributor for the Champ HP3 computerized home blender that far surpasses all the competition. The most powerful, the longest warranty (8 years!), most convenient, and easiest to clean, the Champ HP3 blender will revolutionize your cooking and eating habits.

Bob's Red Mill

5209 S. E. International Way
Milwaukie, OR 97222
1-800-349-2173 Fax: 1-503-653-1339
www.bobsredmill.net

An amazing array of high-quality packaged stone-ground whole grains, seeds, beans, mixes, cereals, and more.

Bragg Live Food Products

Box 7
Santa Barbara, CA 93102
1-800-446-1990
www.bragg.com

Distributor for Bragg Liquid Aminos and Bragg Apple Cider Vinegar. Bragg Liquid Aminos are formulated from non-GMO certified soybeans and purified water. It is not fermented and no table salt is added. A nutritious, better-tasting alternative to tamari and soy sauce (shoyu).

Brown Cow Farm
3810 Delta Fair Boulevard
Antioch, CA 94509
Phone: 1-925-757-9209
Fax: 1-925-757-9160
www.browncowfarm.com
Email: info@browncowfarm.com

Creamiest texture yogurt on the planet. Even the nonfat yogurt tastes and feels creamy. Made from milk from Jersey herds that have never been treated with r-BST (bovine growth hormone), Brown Cow yogurts contain live active cultures and they do NOT contain refined sugars, gelatin, modified food starches or whey protein concentrates. Delicious!

Celestial Seasonings
4600 Sleepytime Drive
Boulder, CO 80301-3292

Manufacturer of every imaginable herbal tea blend.

Eden Foods, Inc.
701 Tecumseh Road
Clinton, MI 49236
Phone: 1-888-441-EDEN (3336)
1-888-424-EDEN
International: 1-517-456-7424
Fax: 1-517-456-7025/1-517-456-7854
www.edenfoods.com

Eden Foods offers nutritious, certified organic foods including barley malt sweetener, beans, pastas, soymilk, condiments, oils, and snack foods.

Ener-G® Foods, Inc.
P.O. Box 84487
Seattle, WA 98124-5787
1-800-331-5222
www.ener-g.com

Manufacturer of egg-replacer, a gluten-free, cholesterol-free, lactose-free vegan egg substitute used as a leavening agent. It contains various starches and is not nutritionally comparable to eggs.

Hain Celestial Group
734 Franklin Avenue #444
Garden City, NY 11530
1-800-SOY-MILK (769-6455)
www.hain-celestial.com
www.westsoy.com

This group includes Westbrae, Westsoy, Hain, and several other natural food companies. Their excellent organic, non-GMO products include soymilk, healthy snack foods, pastas, soups, beans, oils, and condiments.

Imagine Foods, Inc.
1245 San Carlos Avenue
San Carlos, CA 94070
1-650-565-6300
www.imaginefoods.com
Email: questions@imaginefoods.com

Imagine Foods offers a variety of organic beverages, desserts, soups and broths including dairy-free, soy-free, corn-free, vegan, and kosher products.

International Gourmet Specialties Company
180 E. Broad Street
Columbus, OH 43215
1-800-727-8260
www.classico.com

Distributor for Classico pasta sauces. Classico sauces contain no preservatives, and most are very low in fat (only olive oil is used), gluten-free, and without added sweeteners. The flavors and ingredients are pure and authentic, unlike much of the "competition."

Jane's Kitchen

P. O. Box 2271
Harrison, AR 72602
1-870-743-9328
www.cavendersseasoning.com

Distributor for Cavender's Greek Seasoning, a perfect blend of 13 different spices. Available in original and salt-free. Cavender's improves almost any savory dish.

Kashi® Company

P.O. Box 8557
La Jolla, CA 92038-8557
www.Kashi.com

Distributor of pesticide-free whole grain cereals, very low in fat and sugars.

Lee Kum Kee, Inc.

304 South Date Avenue
Alhambra, CA 91803
www.LKK.com

Manufacturer of Chinese condiments, including hoisin sauce and vegetarian stir-fry sauce.

Lundberg Family Farms

5370 Church Street
Richvale, CA 95974-0369
Phone: 1-916-882-4551   Fax: 1-916-882-4500
www.lundberg.com

A huge variety of rice, rice cakes, and rice syrups. Lundberg's rice is grown and processed in accordance with the family's commitment to the land and environment, and their products are unsurpassed in flavor and nutrition.

Miyako Oriental Foods, Inc.

4287 Puente Avenue
Baldwin Park, CA 91706
Phone: 1-626-962-9633 Fax: 1-626-814-4569
www.coldmountainmiso.com

Miyako produces various kinds of miso, all made from 100% certified organic non-GMO soybeans.

Mori-Nu Tofu

2050 W. 190th Street, Suite 110
Torrance, CA 90504
Phone: 1-310-787-0200
Fax: 1-310-787-2727
www.morinu.com

Mori-Nu produces silken Lite tofu, the world's lowest-fat tofu. Its aseptic packaging keeps it fresh without refrigeration or preservatives. Available in soft, firm, and extra firm, Mori-Nu's silken texture is ideal for desserts, smoothies, spreads, and baked goods, but is not always interchangeable with regular water-packed tofu.

Mrs. Leeper's Pasta, Inc.

12455 Kerran Street, Suite 200
Poway, CA 92064-6855
1-858-486-1101
Fax: 1-858-486-5115
www.mrsleepers.com

Manufacturer of quality, organic pastas, including a wheat-free, gluten-free line of pastas.

Purity Foods, Inc.

2871 W. Jolly Road
Okemos, MI 48864
www.purityfoods.com

Organic and natural food products, including the Vita-Spelt line of spelt pastas and flours, grains, beans, and dried fruits.

Red Star Yeast and Products

A Division of Universal Foods Corporation
P.O. Box 737
Milwaukee, WI 53202
1-414-271-6755
www.redstaryeast.net

Producers of Red Star nutritional yeast specifically developed for vegetarians, containing minerals and a reliable source of vitamin B_{12}.

Sucanat® North America Corporation

26 Clinton Drive #117
Hollis, NH 03049
Phone: 1-603-595-2922
Fax: 1-603-595-2923
www.wholesomesweeteners.com

Sucanat® (sugar cane natural) is a natural sweetener derived from 100% evaporated sugar cane juice. Sucanat® is granulated and unrefined, retaining the vitamins, minerals, and trace elements found in the sugar cane plant. Use just as you would regular sugar. Preferred for cereals, baked goods, and desserts.

Tree of Life, Inc.

405 Golfway West Drive
St. Augustine, FL 32095
1-800-260-2424
www.treeoflife.com

Natural, organic, and specialty foods specialists. Products include soymilk made from "The Better Bean" (which is more easily digested), organic frozen berries and vegetables, soyburgers, and organic tofu products, such as smoked tofu, in various flavors.

Vitasoy

400 Oyster Point Boulevard,
Suite 201
South San Francisco, CA 94080

1-800-VITASOY
www.vitasoy-usa.com
Manufacturer of a wide variety of tofu and other soy-based products, including Nayonaise, soymilk, dressings, and more.

White Wave, Inc.

1990 N. 57th Court
Boulder, CO 80301
www.whitewave.com
www.SilkIsSoy.com

Manufacturers of delicious products all made from organic soybeans. Tofu, tempeh, baked tofu, soymilk, and Silk cultured soy yogurt—the all-time best-tasting, creamiest, most delicious cultured soy yogurt ever created.

Yves Veggie Cuisine

1638 Derwent Way
Delta, BC V3M 6R9
Canada
1-800-667-9837
www.yvesveggie.com

Manufacturer of cholesterol-free, low-fat, and fat-free soy-based meat analogues. Delicious, satisfying, and free of preservatives, artificial ingredients, and animal products, Yves products will amaze and delight even the pickiest eater.

MEASUREMENT CONVERSIONS:

U.S.		Milliliters	
1	teaspoon	5	milliliters
2	teaspoons	10	
1	tablespoon (4 tsp.)	14	
2	tablespoons	28	
¼	cup (4 Tbsp.)	56	
½	cup	120	
¾	cup	170	
1	cup	240	
1¼	cups	280	
1½	cups	340	
2	cups	450	
2¼	cups	500	(½ liter)
2½	cups	560	
3	cups	675	
3½	cups	750	
4	cups (1 quart)	900	
4½	cups	1000	(1 liter)
5	cups	1120	

OVEN TEMPERATURE CONVERSIONS:

Fahrenheit	Celsius	Gas Mark
225 degrees	110 degrees	¼
250	130	½
275	140	1
300	150	2
325	170	3
350	180	4
375	190	5
400	200	6
425	220	7
450	230	8
475	240	9
500	250	10

EQUIVALENTS FOR INGREDIENTS:

cilantro Chinese parsley, fresh coriander
black-eyed peas cowpeas
scallion spring onion, green onion
tofu soybean curd
zucchini courgettes, marrow
baking soda sodium bicarbonate
vanilla extract vanilla essence
bell pepper capsicum
soy sauce soya sauce, shoyu
eggplant aubergine
Roma tomatoes plum tomatoes
arugula rocket, roquette
won bok Napa cabbage, Chinese cabbage
zest rind (of citrus fruit)
hazelnut filbert
mesclun mixed baby greens
chickpeas garbanzo beans
almond extract almond essence

PASTA EQUIVALENTS:

farfalle bow ties
rotini corkscrew
fusilli spirals
conchiglie shells
capellini angel hair
rotelle little wheels

SHOPPING (WHERE TO FIND STUFF)

Now that you have the recipes, where do you buy the ingredients? Unfortunately, not all of the foods and ingredients in this cookbook can be found at your local supermarket. The adventure begins with The Food Hunt, a shopping excursion beyond the usual. Here are some suggestions about where to look for certain, less familiar items. If you can't find them locally, please refer to the Resources list at the end of the book for a list of companies and their websites. They can help you locate their products in your area, or provide online ordering services.

HEALTH/NATURAL FOOD STORE

Bragg Liquid Aminos
Barlean's flaxseed oil (refrigerator)
Flaxseed meal (Bob's Red Mill)
Organic produce
Soymilk
Kashi® cereal
Lundberg's rice cakes
Ener-G® egg replacer
Arrowroot powder
Vegenaise®
Better Than Milk powdered soymilk
Sucanat®
Brown rice syrup
Barley malt sweetener
Natural nut butters
Tahini
Naan
Pita
Miso (refrigerator)
Yves soy-based fat-free deli slices ("fake meat")
Tofu (refrigerator)

Mori-Nu silken tofu (aseptic box on shelf)
Organic apple juice

ASIAN MARKET

Rice paper wrappers
Hoisin sauce
Vegetarian stir-fry sauce
Thai hot sauce
Dark sesame oil
Tapioca (beads or pearls)
Rice (exotic varieties)
Rice noodles (also called rice stick)
Chinese wheat noodles
Bean thread
Tofu
Mung bean sprouts (fresh)
Fresh herbs and greens
Exotic mushrooms (canned and fresh)
Nori
Kombu
Dulse
Ginger root
Garlic
Herbs

GOURMET SHOP/MIDDLE EASTERN DELI

Olives (Kalamata and other varieties)
Greek-style yogurt (extra-thick)
Pita
Cheeses made from goat's and sheep's milk
Unusual beans
Tahini
Seasonings and condiments

COSTCO/SAM'S CLUB

Organic baby greens
Spinach
Romaine
Extra virgin olive oil

Capers
Sun-dried tomatoes
Balsamic vinegar
Classico pasta sauces
Almonds
Walnuts
Pecans
Macadamia nuts
Dried cranberries
Raisins
Prunes
Chèvre (goat cheese)
Feta (sheep's milk cheese)
Sun-dried tomatoes
Red, yellow, orange bell peppers

FARMERS' MARKET

Seasonal, locally grown fresh fruits and vegetables
Organic, local produce

BULK BINS

Nutritional yeast flakes (Red Star)
Date pieces (small bits dusted with oat flour)
Oat bran

Organic pastas (including orzo)
Soba noodles
Almonds
Walnuts
Pumpkin seeds (pepitas)
Sunflower seeds
Buckwheat flour
Whole wheat pastry flour
Whole wheat flour
Other flours (spelt, garbanzo, soy, unbleached, etc.)
Rolled oats
Rolled barley, triticale, rye, etc.
Rice (all varieties and blends)
Beans (garbanzo, mung, pinto, navy, kidney, black, etc.)
Lentils, split peas
Quinoa
Millet
Wheatberries
Kamut
Barley
Vegetarian chili mix
Polenta (coarse cornmeal)